CONTENTS

A CAUSE WORTH LIVING FOR

The story of former terrorist David Hamilton

DAVID T HAMILTON

10 Publishing
a division of **10** of those.com

British Library Cataloguing in Publication Data

A record for this book is available from the British Library

ISBN: 978-1-913278-96-0

Designed by Mike Thorpe

Printed in Denmark by Nørhaven

10Publishing, a division of 10ofthose.com

Unit C, Tomlinson Road, Leyland, PR25 2DY, England

Email: info@10ofthose.com

Website: www.10ofthose.com

FOREWORD

There are countless exciting stories of liberation from drug addiction and bondage, which glorify the grace of Almighty God. In my years of work for Teen Challenge, I have had the privilege to have heard many of these testimonials. The story of David Hamilton is at the level of Nicky Cruz and other special conversions. I believe that the reader – like me – will be gripped, moved and inspired by David's amazing change from hatred to love, from a devilish terrorist in Northern Ireland to an evangelist in the Army of Jesus Christ!

During my travels all over Europe I have heard countless stories of the work of David Hamilton. God uses him in a unique way to reach prisoners and drug users, ordinary people on the streets and schoolchildren, with the gospel. The Christians in the Churches are touched by the anointing of the Holy Spirit on his life and inspired to see him serve unconditionally in the service of Jesus Christ.

Don Wilkerson
Executive Director
Teen Challenge
International Fellowship

PREFACE

It is now over 25 years since I first published by book, telling the story of how God broke into my life while lying in a prison cell. I thank God my little book has enjoyed a wide circulation across Europe as well as the United Kingdom.

I am delighted a fresh printing – the fourth – of the British edition has been undertaken by 10ofthose.com, to whose ministry so many are indebted. We share the same goal for many to be made aware how God can change lives and to show there is no such thing as a hopeless case.

About the author

Since prison, David has worked for Prison Fellowship (5 years) and then directed the work of Teen Challenge in N. Ireland (2 Years). He was asked to become the national Evangelist for Teen Challenge in the UK and moved to Wales to set up the Teen Challenge School of Evangelism. While living there he was ordained as an Evangelist with the Apostolic Church in Great Britain. He next spent ten years of extensive travel around Europe as an international evangelist with Eurasia Teen Challenge before settling in Manchester in 1998. He founded a charity, "Life Challenge" and opened a drug rehabilitation centre, dealing with teens and young adults addressing their life-controlling problems. Through this ministry many young men and women have been successfully delivered from drugs and alcohol addiction. In 2004 he took up a full-time pastorate at a church in Stockport, Manchester. Since retiring from the pastorate (2014) he continues to have an itinerant ministry across the U.K.

David and his wife Sharon have returned home to live in Northern Ireland again, he may be contacted through his publisher, 10ofthose.com.

DEDICATIONS

This book is dedicated to the three most important women in my life:

My spiritual grandmother, Annie Beggs, who prayed me into the Kingdom of God, to whom I am eternally thankful.

My mother, Christina Hamilton, for her love and devotion to her husband and family for whom her prayers have been unceasing.

Last but not least, to my wife Sharon. Of all God's gifts graciously bestowed upon me, she is the one I cherish most truly a jewel of great price!

Chapter One

BORN A PROTESTANT

I was born on a cold frosty morning, in the winter of 1956, in Cookstown, Co. Tyrone. As the midwife tended to my mother, my father was busy outside in the yard trying to thaw out the pump to draw some water. It was frozen solid, and what little water he got was quickly brought inside and placed on the stove. Even though the delivery went well, there was still much concern. I was six weeks premature, and weighed in at just 3 lb 8 oz. I was quickly bundled up in warm blankets to keep out the bitter cold and rushed off to the hospital. There I stayed for the next three weeks, and only when I reached the grand weight of 5 lb was it deemed safe to allow me home.

My earliest recollection of childhood was my first day at school. I can recall playing in the sand-pit, and as I looked up I saw my mother's worried face looking through the window of the door. Only when I smiled at her did she turn to walk away, while wiping a tear away from her eye. Perhaps my fondest memory of those early days were my regular visits to my uncle's workshop. He was the town shoemaker. After school, I would run the hundred yards to his workshop, which was situated at the back of the main shop. When I entered through the gate, I was always aware of the smell of the leather. Most times I would find him sitting on a wooden stool, with a boot or shoe held between his knees. He would look up to see who had come in, and as always, he would greet me with a smile.

Usually he would have a mouthful of small nails and a hammer in his hand. I would watch him swing the hammer to his mouth, pick up a single nail and drive it home into the sole of the shoe. As always, the nails were in perfect alignment, equally spaced apart. I was always amazed and wondered why he never hit himself with the hammer.

"Can I have a try?" I would ask, but he would just smile and give me a pat on the head, "Maybe when you're older." From that time on I had a desire to work with leather, but little did I know then, where I would later learn my leather-craft; it would be in Belfast jail.

Like any young family we got up to all kinds of mischief. I remember once my oldest sister Joy, who was nine years old at the time, decided to make toffee for us when my mother was not at home. She went into the kitchen and poured sugar into a pan and put it on the cooker. I do not know what else she added but whatever it was, the toffee tasted nothing like the toffee I bought; it was awful. I did not want to eat it, but my big sister insisted I did. My mother arrived home to find me in tears, complaining of a sore tummy.

My mother arrived home to find me in tears, complaining of a sore tummy.

"It must have been something you've eaten," she said as she rubbed my tummy. I hadn't the nerve to tell her. I knew that look in my big sister's eye; if I dared to tell Mum I would have been in worse trouble when I went to bed later on.

When I was eight years old, our family moved to another town called Omagh, but I do not recall having many memories from living there. One year later we moved home again because of my father's work. This time it was to a large housing estate on the outskirts of Belfast called Rathcoole. Back then it had a population of 14,000, and was believed to be one of the largest housing projects in all of Europe. In our street, which consisted of ten houses, half were occupied by Roman Catholic families, many of whom were my friends. I can recall playing football together on the field opposite our house. One of the boys playing at that time was called Bobby Sands. Little did any of us know then that we would all be affected by the Troubles that were shortly to break out in Northern Ireland, that we would be no longer friends, and some of us would even become enemies. Nor did we know then that both Bobby and I, and quite a few others there would end up in prison as political prisoners, some as Republicans and others like me as Loyalists. Bobby went on to lead the hunger strike protest in the Maze prison, in which he was the first to die.

Northern Ireland has been embroiled in deadly political fighting for 300 years. There are two separate Irelands. The Republic of Ireland consists of 26 counties. More than 90 percent of its people are Catholic. Northern Ireland is made up of six counties in north-eastern Ireland. Most of the inhabitants of the counties, which cover two-thirds of the ancient province of Ulster, are Protestants because of colonisation by England in the seventeenth century. The English confiscated the land of Ulster from local chieftains and divided the acreage among thousands of Protestant

English and Scottish settlers who regarded the "native" Irishmen with a mixture of contempt, fear, and desire for their manual labour. The immigration of Protestants into a mostly Catholic land created a lasting division between Protestants and Catholics, and it aggravated the natural conflict between rich and poor and landowners and tenants.

Some Catholics in Northern Ireland still fight for political union with the rest of Ireland. In a united Ireland, Catholics would comprise the vast majority. For that reason, Protestants in the north continue to resist the reunification of the country.

The bitter division between Protestants and Catholics escalated this century. In 1921, five years after the Easter uprising in Dublin, Britain recognised the two separate Irelands. Armed irregulars of the Irish Republican Army (IRA) threatened raids into the north to force the six counties to join the Republic. Northern Ireland resisted strongly and stepped up efforts to guarantee Protestant rule. The government passed laws that made it legal to arrest people on simple suspicion of belonging to illegal organisations, and laws that established curfews and barred the entry of any undesirable person into the six counties. A heavily armed special part-time police force, called the B Specials, was created to assist the Royal Ulster Constabulary (RUC) in keeping the peace.

Protestants ruled the parliament and controlled every aspect of daily life. They were given preference in jobs and housing. Such inequalities kept alive the spirit of rebellion among Republicans who maintained close ties with the IRA in the south. From the 1930s to the 1950s the IRA carried out many sporadic attacks on police barracks and other targets in the north.

A serious assault on Protestant rule of the north came in 1969 when Protestant extremists attacked 500 demonstrators marching from Belfast to Londonderry. IRA recruitment soared as Republicans feared Protestant attacks in all counties. The British government was forced to send 3,000 soldiers to Northern Ireland in July 1969 on a peacekeeping mission. Widespread rioting, brutal raids and the now familiar cycle of terrorism, reprisal, and more terrorism took a heavy toll on both civil liberties and lives. The Catholic Nationalists saw the British army as an occupational force, and the IRA was fighting a war on two sides now, not only against the British army but also the Protestant paramilitary organisations that had been born in the conflict.

One of the incidents instrumental in discolouring my view of Roman Catholics, happened when I was about nine or ten years of age.

One of the incidents I believe that was instrumental in discolouring my view of Roman Catholics, happened when I was about nine or ten years of age. I had a Catholic friend called Jim, and his father had a car. Occasionally I would walk down to the Roman Catholic chapel to meet them coming out just to get a ride home in their car. I remember a particular Sunday as I was standing waiting.

My friend came out alone, "We have to walk home," he said.

"Why?" I asked.

"My Father has to go to an IRA meeting," was his reply.

Then it meant nothing to me as I had never heard of the IRA before. But years later that conversation came back to me when I was involved in the tartan gang KAI. I went back to that Catholic chapel again, this time with the gang, around seventy of us, to burn the place down. Only when the police arrived in force and a full-scale riot began, was the chapel saved.

My first awareness of the political difference between Protestant and Roman Catholics happened when I was fourteen years of age. That day I had been skiving off school and was with a group of other boys, who were all Catholics.

I stood there listening as they began to discuss among themselves what they should do to me.

We were down in the glen, where amongst the trees we had a swing made from a rope attached to a branch that jutted out over the river. I stood there listening as they began to discuss among themselves what they should do to me. They then beat me up and threw me into the river. As I climbed back out of the water, I was still trying to figure out what it was I had done to deserve this beating.

I had to ask them why they did this, and one of them gave me the reason. It was because I was a Protestant and they were all Catholics. Until then I did not know what a Loyalist or a Republican was, or that there was a difference between Protestants and Catholics.

That day was a turning point in my young life, sadly in the wrong direction. I decided never again would I have a Catholic friend, only Protestant. I also made another decision to join a gang – it was much safer to be a gang member.

So it was that day David Hamilton, like so many others among the youth, became a victim of the Troubles in Northern Ireland. He was too young then to ever imagine the price he would pay or the consequences he would suffer for making that choice. But back then he thought it was the wisest and safest thing to do.

Chapter Two

RATHCOOLE KAI

I was one of the first members of a Tartan gang that was formed in the early 1970s as Protestants armed themselves as vigilantes protecting their own areas from IRA attacks. Street fighting broke out almost every night. Every neighbourhood had its own gang until many of the gangs in Rathcoole combined into a single large gang of around two hundred approximately. We became known as the notorious Rathcoole KAI. Tragically, the letters K-A-I stood for 'Kill All Irishmen.' We even formed a flute-band and began to march on the twelfth of July parade. We were Ulstermen and proud to be British.

Protestant families would wake up to find their Catholic neighbours had left quietly during the night.

We began to terrorise Catholics in the area where we lived. At first, we only smashed windows in their houses. Later, we made petrol bombs and set the Catholic school on fire; many homes of Catholics were also attacked in this way. Back then I thought this was the right thing to do, it would make our area much safer, if it was all Protestant.

Soon most of the Catholics left Rathcoole for their own safety. "Midnight flits" were common, Protestant families would wake up to find their next-door Catholic neighbours had left quietly during the night. Many Protestants who lived in Catholic areas in the city were also forced out of their homes and many moved into Rathcoole to live. My mother cried when our next door neighbours, a Catholic family, decided it best to move to an all-Catholic neighbourhood in another part of Belfast.

The same aggressive attacks were happening to Protestants and Catholics who were living in mixed estates all over Northern Ireland, as each side wanted supremacy. Soon Rathcoole became known as one of the biggest Protestant strongholds in the north of Ireland. It is still the same today. Ulster flags fly all the year round. Many walls and footpaths are painted red, white, and blue. Rathcoole was and still is a "no-go" area for Catholics. Workmen entering the area have been murdered just because they were thought to be Catholic, but were in fact, Protestant. These kinds of killings are carried out by both sides.

He walked up to her, put his arm around her, and said, "I'm going to shoot you."

A lady called Pearl McKeown, who worked with me in Prison Fellowship, would often share the story of how her daughter Karen was shot in the throat in the car park of her church. The gunman lurked in the darkness; his only aim was to kill a Protestant, man or woman, he didn't care. When Karen came out of her church he walked up to her, put his arm around her, and said, "I'm going to shoot you." Karen laughed, thinking it was a boy from church playing a joke on her. Then he pulled the trigger. She died a few weeks later in a hospital.

Back then, these senseless killings were seen as the thing to do. Each side reacting in a 'Tit for Tat' murder, with an innocent Protestant or Roman Catholic becoming the next statistic of the Troubles in Northern Ireland.

Against this backdrop of murder and fear, I began my teenage years. Even at school I began to get a name for being crazy when it came to fighting. How this came about was more by accident than anything else, because in fact I acted out of fear rather than temper. Like all schools we had our share of bullies. One of these guys was a huge skinhead called Norny. I had seen him on several occasions picking on guys and just roughing them up. A few weeks had passed before he noticed that I was the new kid on the block.

One day I was walking up a narrow corridor on my way to class. The corridor was packed with pupils waiting to go into classrooms as soon as the bell went to allow them in. Directly in front of me I saw Norny step out, as I passed him by he immediately jumped onto my back and shouted, "Give me a ride!" I was expecting him to do something. I simply stopped dead and tossed him over my shoulder; he tumbled onto the floor like a sack of coal. Everyone started to laugh, except Norny and me. He started to see red and began to shout what he was going to do to me. I decided not to hang around, and took off down the corridor with Norny close on my heels. There was really nowhere safe to go, so I turned and ran into a classroom, unfortunately it was empty. Seconds later Norny came through the door as well. He was pleased to see just me standing there at the front of the blackboard. As he slowly came towards me I looked around for something to use as a weapon. Suddenly I saw a wooden blackboard compass and grabbed it. Norny laughed. "What are you going to do with that?" he asked.

I told him, "If you lift your hand to hit me I'll stick it in you!"

He laughed again and made a dash toward me. I let him have it straight into his stomach; he gave a scream and fell to the floor clutching his belly. The compass was still embedded in him. There wasn't much blood that I could see, but they took him to hospital anyway. It was the talk of the whole school. Rumours flying around the place that I had knifed Big Norny and left him for dead in the classroom!

At the time this happened I just turned and ran out and went to my class, as if nothing had happened. I honestly wasn't worried by the whole thing; it was his own fault, he asked for it. Ten minutes later the police came in and took me out (the police station was actually next door to the college). I was cautioned and sent home, nothing ever came of it. Norny and his bully friends never gave me any bother at school from that day on. He was known as 'the bully with two belly buttons' after that!

After the incident with Big Norny I had begun to carry a weapon. I would never go anywhere without a blade. Not that I restricted myself to just using a knife; if the need arose I'd use anything I could as a weapon. Our gang activities were not confined to Rathcoole either. Most of my Saturdays were spent in Belfast city centre. At that time in the early seventies, the tartan gangs were big all over Northern Ireland.

Each Saturday all the Protestant gangs would rendezvous at a certain place in or around the city centre. We would run riot around the streets until we found the Catholic tartan gangs and then all hell broke loose. Many times, some of us would end up spending the night in the police cells. I never complained; others would spend their evening in the Royal Victoria Hospital. I have even known a few gang members to die in these gang wars.

Once I was with members of the KAI gang down in Newcastle in a night club. I was sitting in a bar drinking with my girlfriend. I got up and went to the toilet; when I returned this guy was sitting up tight beside her with his arm around her and trying to kiss her, and she was struggling to keep him off. As I came back to my seat I casually asked him if he would like to kiss me. As he was rising up out of his seat I smashed a pint glass over his head and left him lying in a cocktail of blood and beer. Suddenly one of his mates hit me on the back of the head from behind and knocked me across a table. As I got up, I grabbed a bottle from of the table and when he ran at me I smashed it over his head. I was still holding the neck of the broken bottle in my hand when a third guy attacked me from the side. I turned and caught him by the back of his hair and plunged the bottleneck up into his face. I heard him scream and when I looked at him his nose was gone! A fourth man started to approach me, but when he saw the state of his friend's face he soon changed his mind, and shaking his hands and head he began to back off.

Many times some of us would end up spending the night in the police cells.

I was saturated with blood all down the front of me. I ran out of the lounge and into the toilets of the club. I saw someone I knew and he took off a large woollen jumper and I put it over my t-shirt. A short time later, the police rushed in; I was standing amongst the crowd. They stood in the middle of the dance floor. "Can you see him here?" one of the police officers asked.

This guy looked around the crowd, when he saw me he stopped and stared at me. I just stared back at him. He knew I had been involved in the fight earlier. He then said, "No, I don't see him." They turned and went out again. The waitress also knew it was me but decided it was in her own best interests to stay quiet. I have never set foot in that night club since that night, yet twelve years later in Belfast I was talking to a stranger and he reminded me of this incident – it turned out he was one of the bar staff in question. I asked him how he had remembered the incident and how he knew I was the one involved; he answered, "It's not every day you see someone having their nose cut off, is it?"

Another time a large number of the gang went by train to an Orange parade in Londonderry. As the parade was planning to cross over the bridge into a prominent Catholic area, a huge Catholic crowd had gathered on the other side of the bridge to try and stop this from happening. Again, as all mayhem broke loose, the Security Forces charged in to try and separate the two sides. I remember seeing army personnel carriers (known as 'pigs') touching toe to tail across the whole breadth of the bridge, then two suddenly parted and all these 'squaddies' (soldiers) in full riot gear came charging towards us.

"It's not every day you see someone having their nose cut off, is it?"

What amused me was the sight of an actual fire-fighting engine driving towards us. I couldn't believe what I was seeing. Soldiers clung from the side of it. I'd never seen anything like this before in any riot situation – what were they planning to do with that? I asked myself. I didn't have to wait long to find out; as it drew closer they suddenly started to blast the cannon at us. I laughed out loud – they were using it as a huge water pistol! We carried on rioting. We weren't afraid on getting a soaking. Some of the guys started dancing around under the huge spraying arc thinking it was hilarious until we realised it wasn't just water it was firing, it was blue dye. Everyone was turning blue. It was one thing being soaked wet but another thing to be dyed blue!

Next thing I felt something strike me on my right shoulder, spinning me around; it took my breath away with the surge of pain. Suddenly I was in a lot more pain. It took me only a moment to realise what had happened. I had been shot with a rubber bullet; it was there lying beside me. I picked it up before retreating to safety.

It didn't end for the rest of the day. The army and police continued to arrest anybody covered in blue dye, loads of guys and some girls too were being grabbed and thrown into the back of these 'army pigs' or 'paddy wagons' (slang for police vans used then) and we were all charged with riotous behaviour. It took weeks for that dye to wash off. Later that evening we were all escorted by the police to the train station and put on a train for Belfast. Of course, that train was trashed. There was not a single window left in place, and some of the guys were actually sitting on the top of the train drinking while it was hammering along. I don't know if we lost anyone, or if anyone was killed by falling off. It was a miracle we made it home in one piece. I sat quiet most of the journey home suffering a lot of pain, and I still had the rubber bullet inside my jacket pocket – a nice souvenir from my day trip to Derry!

It was during these times as a gang member as I was running around different areas of Belfast that I ended up being shot. Often I stayed up the Shankill Road for three or four days without going home. The Shankill Road is an area that is seen by many Loyalists as the heart of Protestantism. I thought it was safe enough because I was known by many of the Shankill Tartan gang members. But I was naïve, young and foolish. The night I got shot I was in a house that gang members often stayed in. A gang member informed me he was ordered to do a punishment shooting, known as a knee-capping (this was done by shooting petty thieves or consistent joy riders, as a form of punishment, in the area of the knee or lower leg, or sometimes both knees, depending on the seriousness of their crime.) He asked me to go along with him, as it was risky being alone. So I said, "OK."

Ten minutes later we were standing on a street corner. My job, I thought, was to watch out for the Security Forces. As I turned around to ask him who was the target to be. He answered, "You!" and lifted up the gun towards my face. Thankfully I was standing quite close to him. I immediately reached up and grabbed his arm which held the gun. As I pulled his hand down, the gun went off. I heard three very loud bangs in quick succession and for a moment I thought I was deaf. All I could hear was the ringing in my ears. I fell to the ground and as I looked up at him he leaned over and pushed the gun towards my face again. He pulled the trigger and nothing happened. The gun had jammed! He then turned and started running away up the street.

I felt a burning sensation in my foot and leg. I looked but could see nothing wrong. But when I kicked my shoe off I saw blood escaping everywhere. I was bleeding in three different places. I could not put my foot back down on the ground and stood holding on to a lamp post. Some neighbours came out to investigate the shots. They carried me into a club across the street and laid me on a pool table.

They carried me into a club across the street and laid me on a pool table.

After a few minutes a stranger arrived and examined me. He spoke authoritatively, "He needs to go to the hospital or he could bleed to death. He has possibly three bullets in him." The man quickly put me in a car and took me to a hospital that thankfully was only a few miles away. He carried me into the hospital over his shoulder and laid me on a stretcher. "This young lad has been shot," he said, and turned around and walked out.

The police soon arrived to question me about my gunshot wounds. The officer asked me my name and where I lived. "Why do you need my name?" I asked. The grumpy officer said, "We need to inform your parents and get their permission to operate." I was concerned about my mother who had a heart condition. I thought, "If she hears I've been shot, she surely will have a heart attack." The officer tried to reassure me that they had ways of breaking such news to people but I wasn't convinced. He then became annoyed with me and began to shout, "Listen to me, boy, I want your name and I want it right now. Otherwise, you're in big trouble."

"OK," I said, "My name is Francis McFrancis."

The policeman left to talk to the hospital staff. I decided it was also time for me to leave. I got up and hopped across the room and cautiously opened the door just enough to peer out at the corridor to see if any other police were around. The way seemed clear and I hopped along the corridor and breathed a sigh of relief as I made it around the corner. "Almost free," I thought. The next thing I heard was the sound of heavy boots running down the corridor.

"Where do you think you're going?" the voice of my friendly policeman boomed. I knew he was glad to see me because he led me back to my little room and placed a screw outside to keep me company.

Some of my gang friends came to see me the next day. When they tried to slip into my room, the *"Where do you think, you're going?" the voice of my friendly policeman boomed.* policeman asked them, "And where do you lot think you're going to?" They replied, "We're here to see a patient." He asked, "And who might that be?" One of my friends shouted back, "Davey Hamilton."

"OK, thank you," he said, as he wrote my identity down in his little black book.

I remember coming out of the operating room on a trolley. As I passed through the swinging doors I looked up and there were my parents standing there. I shall never forget the anguish on my mother's face. My father had his arm around her shoulder, trying to console her. When I saw her I began to cry too. I showed her the two bullets that the doctor let me keep. Today I carry the third bullet still in my foot. The doctor thought it would do more damage to remove the bullet than to allow it to remain in my foot. It is a constant reminder to me that bullets can kill.

I don't know how true it was but I was told later by a friend that some of the other gang members had taken offence that I was wearing the KAI gang colours on their turf so they decided to shoot me. So I learned it was not safe to go outside your own area; best to stay in your own hood; it was always strangers who got murdered. "Don't trust anyone," was the motto of the day.

Chapter Three

JOINING THE RANKS

When the Troubles escalated, vigilantes were formed to protect their own areas, which is how the Paramilitaries came into being. One night these men came to talk to the gang leaders (there were still a few little gangs that had not amalgamated with the others into the KAI). They suggested all the Protestant gangs become one as an army, and they would train us as soldiers. That was exactly what we did.

For me, this was when my training as a terrorist began. We were issued with army combat clothing, and eventually began to be trained with various weapons.

In the early seventies, there was much rioting on the streets of Northern Ireland. Rathcoole had its share of it. There were riots quite frequently. Once during one of these riots we attacked an army patrol and tried to steal the weapon off a soldier as he lay on the ground. The gun was attached to his wrist by a strap. We were unable to detach it but grabbed the magazine from out of the weapon and ran away to avoid being captured.

But it wasn't long before I was arrested and ended up being interrogated in the local police barracks. It came about because I had been on sentry duty outside the local pub the night before, we had a security rota operating to protect the place from being bombed. I slept late the following morning but as I woke up in bed I knew I would be in big trouble if I didn't get the gun back to the place where some of our weapons were kept. I got dressed and put the gun down the waistband of my trousers. I pulled on a denim jacket before going downstairs and checked in the mirror to make sure the gun could not be seen. Memories were fresh in my mind about an incident a month or so before when I had brought a gun into the house. I had been so sure that even if the police raided our house again they would never find the gun. Much to my surprise my mother found it and went berserk! She was shouting and crying at the same time. She said if I ever killed anyone it would be her death too.

I argued back. "We are at war with the IRA. Someone has to fight them. The police and army are restrained because of red tape. Their hands are tied."

"I don't care," she replied, "Murder is murder no matter what. I could not live with the knowledge that you had killed someone's son and left a mother or a young wife and family mourning."

That was not the end of my problems over bringing a gun into the house. When my father got home and found out, he called me into the front room. When I closed the door and turned around he punched me hard. He grabbed me by the throat, shoved me up against the wall, put his face close to mine and yelled, "As long as you live, never bring another gun into this house." All I could do was nod my head. From then on, I made sure that whenever I carried a gun, I did not bring it home. I knew my old man was serious. When he said something he only said it once. He would have beaten me to a pulp, even though I was 17 and loved fighting.

My dad was the toughest man I knew. He had boxed to the highest level in the British Army. Because he was excellent with a skipping rope they nicknamed him "The Skipper." Even now that he is older, I still would not want to cross him.

Once when the police were interrogating me at the police holding centre in Ladus Drive Belfast, when the detective found out who my father was, he sat back in his chair, I could see he was startled. He immediately turned around and told the other officer sitting beside him not to lay a hand on me. (It was common in those days to receive a beating while in police custody.) The detective went on to say my father would kill him if he thought he had so much as laid a finger on me while questioning me. He told his partner stories about how tough my father was. I just sat there and smiled. I was proud to be Cecil Hamilton's son.

I just sat there and smiled. I was proud to be Cecil Hamilton's son.

I had left the house that morning without any thoughts about robbery or doing anything out of the ordinary. As I walked through the housing estate to what was called "The Diamond" shopping centre, I saw two of my friends, Hughie and Albert, going inside a hardware shop. I crossed the square and walked into the shop behind them. I stopped just inside the door looking around for my mates. They were at the counter being served, and the shopkeeper looked past my friends and stared at me. I saw fear spread across his face as he stared down at my waist. I realised the handle of the gun was protruding from under my jacket. He shouted at the top of his voice, "Don't shoot, don't shoot!"

I didn't know what to do so I turned and ran out of the door. My friends followed and we ran across the square. A few minutes later we sat and talked about what had happened. We thought it was funny. None of us knew just how serious it was. Little did we know we would all end up in prison charged with attempted armed robbery!

When I arrived home that night a heavily armoured police Land Rover was pulling away from my house. Some of the neighbours stood at their gates gossiping, asking what the police were doing at the Hamilton house. I made myself scarce. When it got dark I went back home. My dad met me at the door and told me the police had been looking for me. I told him what had really happened and said that my friends and I had decided to go to Scotland until things cooled down.

Little did we know we would all end up in prison charged with attempted armed robbery!

A few hours later my mate Albert and I stole a car and drove to Larne harbour to catch the ferry. We had found out our mate, Hughie, who had been with us earlier was already arrested and in police custody. So we set off, but hadn't gone far when we heard a police siren. I looked out the rear window and saw the familiar flashing blue lights.

"Hold on," I shouted and pushed the accelerator to the floor. The police were driving a 4x4 Land Rover, it was weighted down with armour, which of course was no match for our stolen car. This was my first police chase. It didn't last very long, we soon left them behind!

It felt pretty good to escape the clutches of the police who were looking for us. We got onto country roads and widened the gap between the police and us. It was obvious that the police had given up hope of catching us, or so I thought.

We sat in a dark farm lane and laughed at how easy it had been to give the police the slip. After an hour we thought it was safe to leave and go on to catch the evening ferry. This time Albert wanted to drive and took the wheel. We had driven only two or three miles when we rounded the bend – straight into a police road block.

"We're caught, Davey!" he screamed.

"Not yet," I replied. "Drive up the grass bank and go around them. There's enough room to pass."

As the car mounted the curb the police officers jumped out of the way.

"We're going to make it, Albert!" I yelled.

Albert was not the world's best driver and swerved all over the road. He lost control and the car veered into a wall on the opposite side of the road and came to a grinding halt. We were only about 300 metres from the police.

"Run Albert!" I shouted. We ran across the back gardens of the nearby homes. I could hear our pursuers close behind.

I jumped into a lily pond to hide. I peered out from the lilies just as policemen with torches ran by. I climbed out of the pond a few minutes later and looked for Albert. When I quietly called out his name his head popped up from inside a rubbish bin. We confidently walked down the street letting on we were locals, until a car suddenly screeched to a halt. "Like a lift, boys?" It was the police and we were caught.

We were put into separate cells at the police station so we could not compare stories. I thought I was hearing things when the officer said Albert and I could not leave unless we confessed to stealing the car. I realised this police station was not aware of the attempted armed robbery charge we were expecting. Albert and I quickly confessed to stealing the car.

We were excited about our unexpected release and were amazed at our luck that no detectives were in the station at the time of our arrest. Otherwise we would have been charged and jailed to await our trial. Shortly we were on board the ferry heading for Scotland. We stayed almost six months in Glasgow, drinking and partying, and going to the Rangers and Celtic football matches. One day I received a letter from my mother telling me that my oldest sister was getting married in a few weeks. I decided to go home for the wedding even though I knew the police were looking for me for other crimes, including a bombing of what we believe to be an undercover army spy-post for gathering intelligence. We were almost killed because the bomb we had planted exploded while we were still in the building. My mate Chuck, who did it with me at the time, was badly burned. I had heard in Scotland that he was in prison awaiting trial for the bombing. This did not put me off going home; I wasn't going to miss my sister's wedding.

As I boarded the ship I decided to get a comfortable seat

down in the lounge. The crossing would take almost four hours, so I planned to sleep for a few hours. As I was ordering a cup of coffee, I saw a young woman in the queue with her back to me. I could not believe my eyes – it was my younger sister Beth. She was thrilled to see me, so we sat and talked throughout the whole trip. This made it seem a lot shorter. I was surprised to learn my mother and father were planning to pick her up after we docked. She told me she had been over in Scotland for a holiday. I can still see the joy on my parents' faces at the ferry port as they saw us both coming down the gang plank. It was a time of great reunion for us all.

My sister's wedding went off really well. Everyone had a great time and were waiting to send Joy and her husband off on their honeymoon. Joy began to cry because she thought surely the police would catch me and send me to jail. She suddenly decided that I should go with them on their honeymoon. I just laughed and refused the offer, much to the relief of her new husband.

I noticed two men standing across the street from the church. They seemed to be interested in the wedding and me in particular. Every time I looked over at them, they looked away. I had my suspicions. I knew I was far enough away that I could easily escape if they chased me. I excused myself and told my sister I wanted to go around behind the church for a smoke. When the men saw me leaving they started running across the street. As soon as I was out of sight I climbed over the hedge surrounding the church. I looked back and saw two faces peeping around the corner of the church. I gave the two plain clothes detectives a friendly wave and I was gone.

The next day I was not so quick. As I walked up to my girlfriend's house, two police officers appeared from nowhere. They each grabbed an arm and walked me down the path to an unmarked car.

I called out to my girlfriend, "Don't worry. I'll be back shortly."

One of the policemen said, "Yeah, don't hold your breath waiting."

I didn't know it then but it would be nine months before I would be back again. Nine months, the length of my first stay in Her Majesty's Prison.

Chapter Four

CRUMLIN ROAD JAIL

The ride to jail I will never forget. I was sitting alone in the back seat of a police car, handcuffed. At first I didn't give it any thought, but the nearer we got to the jail the more quiet I became.

The sombreness of where I was heading landed like a ton of bricks on my shoulders. I realised it might be a long time before I would see Rathcoole again so I made sure I had a good look out of the window to have something to remember.

As the car stopped at the prison gate I looked up at the huge stone-grey walls. It was strange how I saw them in a different way that day. I was not up to visit this time. No, this time I was here to stay! A few moments later the huge double gates swung open to allow us access. The sound of the steel gates closing behind us echoed in my ears. It sounded like thunder.

We sat in the darkness and a cold shudder ran down my spine. I thought, "This is prison. It's not television. This is for real." I heard another heavy rumbling sound as the gates in front of us opened, letting light pour into the tunnel. The car drove slowly across the courtyard and stopped at a sign that read 'Reception.' I was led into the reception area and put into a wooden cubicle to wait for processing.

As I sat there wondering what would happen next, I listened to all the noise. It seemed ages before the bolt on my door was pulled back and an officer with a dark blue overall coat ordered me out. He told me to follow him over to a counter, where he began to write down all my particulars. Afterwards he told an orderly to take us through for a bath. There were other orderlies working there; their uniforms consisted of a blue and white thin stripped shirt and a pair of grey denim trousers.

I noticed one of them had a denim waistcoat on. I found out later on this guy was a long-term prisoner and the other two were short-term prisoners. All the long-term men wore their uniforms tailored to suit themselves, whereas short-term men had to wear whatever they were given to wear. None of them were privileged to wear a waistcoat.

The bathhouse consisted of three cells, 8'x12', each with a half stable door. Inside was a huge cast iron tub, which had lost its white enamel a century before. I searched in vain for a plug, but all I could see was a piece of wood carved out to fit the plug hole. It must have been there a long time because it was well worn, smoothed over the years of constant use. I found out later this was called a 'bung.'

A few minutes later the orderly appeared with a blue towel which he tossed over the door. He set down on the floor a large plastic mug that had a grey knife, fork and spoon in it, a toothbrush, a tube of toothpaste and a bar of soap. After getting dried and dressed again I lifted the mug to examine it – it was disgusting. It had been white many years ago, but was now a dirty cream colour. The inside was worse – it was stained dark brown from the jail tea. Some prisoner had started to carve out his name, it seemed, on the base but had not finished the task. The letters looked crude, hacked out with a razor blade. There was a bottle of bleach upon the window ledge used to clean the bath, so I poured some into my cup. There was an immediate change, the bleach seemed to climb up the inside of the cup. I began to wash the outside of the cup as well. In two minutes, apart from the carvings, you would have thought it was a new mug. I rinsed it off under the hot tap and it was ready for use.

After reception I was led out into what was called the 'basement.' You stay here your first night, before being moved across into one of the wings. When the screw opened the cell door to let me in, I realized there was someone already in it. I expected to be alone. He was an older man, mid-forties I think. I didn't like the look of him. I took the bunk opposite him and never said a word. Eventually I spoke to him, but I soon realized he didn't want to talk; he refused to answer any of my questions, so eventually I caught on and stopped talking. Although he wasn't saying much I was aware he was staring at me, as if trying to weigh me up. I thought to myself, Forget him; he is a weirdo. I was to find out later that night just how much of a weirdo he really was.

I began to concentrate on my surroundings. The walls were painted pink. Seemed very homely! There was a window about eight feet off the ground. If you stood on top of the frame of the iron bed it was possible to pull yourself up by the window bars to look out, not that there was much to see. I lay down on my bed listening to all the strange noises. It seemed doors were being opened and closed far off somewhere, there was also the rattling of keys. As I lay there, I realised that the noise of the doors opening was coming closer to us.

Five minutes later the keys turned in our door, and an orderly stood with a steel bucket. "Do ya want tay? (tea) Dip your mug in the bucket." Another orderly was holding a tray bake; he handed us two bits of square cake, covered in red jam and coconut flake: "Enjoy your supper lads." Before I got a chance to answer, they backed out and the door banged shut again.

I looked in at this strange coloured liquid my mug. Was it tea, coffee or Guinness, a mixture of all three perhaps? It seemed very strong, with the essence of milk. As the night wore on, I listened to conversations going on around us, as other prisoners shouted out through the bars to each other. Eventually things quietened down. The naked light bulb began to flicker. I heard the sound of footsteps coming closer along the landing. The officer or "screw" (slang name for a prison officer, because the old handcuffs they used in prison did not use keys, instead they worked by a screw mechanism) was walking along the landing turning out the lights. The lights were turned out at eleven o'clock each night. Our door flap lifted briefly, and I caught a glimpse of a pair of eyes before we were left totally in the darkness. After our eyes grew accustomed to the dark I just lay and stared at the cell wall, looking at the irregular rectangular shapes formed by the shadow of the iron bars as the moonlight shone through into our cell.

The naked light bulb began to flicker. I heard footsteps coming closer along the landing.

Eventually I fell to sleep. I was awoken suddenly a few hours later by this weirdo. He climbed onto my bed and was standing over me with his pants down playing with himself.

I was mad! I immediately kicked him off, and as he fell on the floor I landed on top of him. I started punching him. He began to scream like a pig! I kept punching until my knuckles were sore. By this time there wasn't a sound from him, just moans, eventually they stopped too. I stood up and looked down at him; I was still angry so I began to kick him until my toes hurt.

The next morning, we were awakened early by a screw and told to "slop-out" – that means to go and empty your chamber-pot. (In those days there were no toilets in the cell). Each man had his own pot. You queued up at the slop house to wash and empty your pot out; the smell of urine hung heavy in the air throughout the prison. He went to walk on but suddenly turned back when he saw the guy's face. It was a mess. "What happened to you?" he asked. He never answered so I said, "He kept falling out of bed during the night onto his face." He was taken away immediately after breakfast to the prison hospital. I never saw him again.

Later on that morning, I was moved over to 'C' Wing. This was a wing for Loyalist prisoners only. After meeting the wing leaders, I was accepted and allowed to stay.

I soon got used to the routine in jail. Many times I watched IRA men on parade from my cell window. While they were out on exercise, they had parade drill just like us, and I saw them having inspections. A well-known Republican leader, now a leading politician, would walk up and down their ranks, talking to individuals. He would then go back into his cell. He seemed to prefer the solitude of his cell. Their orders where given in Gaelic. We even learnt some of these commands.

I had been in jail just a few months when a prison officer outside was murdered by the IRA. The authorities cancelled all prison visits the following day and we were locked in our cells. (At that time, we were entitled to three visits a week because we were on remand and not yet sentenced.) When we were released for supper the leaders decided to riot in protest. Quickly a plan was devised to take over the wing and, if possible, capture some of the screws. When the signal was given, men attacked the few screws who were standing around. Next thing I knew everyone started wrecking the place. Chairs were smashed, table legs were broken off and used as weapons. Prisoners built barricades to prevent the riot squad from coming into the wing.

Next thing I knew everyone started wrecking the place.

For the next few days, prison authorities tried unsuccessfully to regain control of the wing. Alarm bells were continuously ringing. Prisoners were running all over the place arming themselves with all kinds of weapons.

Finally, in desperation, they called in the army. The soldiers smashed their way in through the roof and attacked every prisoner in sight. It was fierce hand-to-hand fighting. It didn't take them long to overpower us, having double the man-power, and firing rubber bullets: we knew we didn't stand a chance.

Some guys locked themselves in cells to try to avoid getting shot or beaten by the soldiers and screws. Afterwards we were stripped naked and handcuffed to the hot water pipe that ran beneath the window just three inches off the floor. Most of the cell doors were broken so the only way they could keep us contained was to handcuff us to the pipe. There we stayed for the next three days until all the doors had been replaced. There was nothing left in our cells. Beds, doors, lockers and chairs had been piled up as barricades. All of which were now piled up with our clothing on the safety wire stretched between the landings; it looked in danger of collapsing at any moment as it hung with a huge sag, about ready to burst.

A few days later I had to make an appearance at court. When I was told to get dressed I asked what clothes I was to wear. "Whatever you find out there, go and find something to put on." I spent an hour searching in the rubble for something to wear. I knew not to ask for an iron. It was weeks before tensions settled and we were allowed back out of our cells again. I didn't know it then, but I would relive this experience a few years later.

Chapter Five

BEHIND THE WIRE

After six months finally I was informed in writing what I was charged with. The usual routine was to be moved down to another prison called Long Kesh to await trial. No one liked the trip down to it. We were put into a vehicle similar to a horse box. We were handcuffed and locked in a cubicle no larger than a dressing-room locker. When you sat down your knees were under the seat of the man in front of you. When the door was shut it was hard not to feel claustrophobic. I heard other men begin to panic as they screamed for their doors to be opened. The screws told them to shut up and be quiet.

When I knew I would be going down, the night before I would try to stay awake reading (by moonlight) and then when my journey started hopefully I would doze off. You could never fall fast asleep; the sway of the truck would stop you. But you could sort of doze a little. By doing this it made the journey seem shorter.

I was put in compound nine, for the remands (those awaiting trial) and this was my home for the next few months. Long Kesh was an old air base from World War II. It was made up of twelve compounds. Each compound was made up of four war-time Nissen huts made of corrugated iron that the prisoners slept in. There was another half-hut used for the toilets and the whole place was surrounded by a galvanised wire fence, about six meters high. On the top of the fence was razor wire, that created the impression of a typical prisoner-of-war camp. The first six compounds consisted of prisoners who were interned.

These were all men the Security Forces suspected of being members of paramilitary organisations. They were arrested and put in jail without any trial, neither did they have a release date of any sort. Some of these men were held for a long time like this. They were known as "the Internees." At least other prisoners had a release date, but not these – they were in limbo!

Life in here was a little better than the Crumlin Road jail. For one thing we had less contact with the screws. Because the policy of Special Category Status to paramilitary prisoners in Northern Ireland's prisons (it did not apply to those in English prisons) was still in existence, Special Category, or political status meant prisoners were treated very much like prisoners of war – they had free association, and arranged their own educational and recreational activities. Neither did they have to wear prison uniforms or do prison work. (It was to be taken away three years later, in 1976.)

We were locked in a wire compound and the screws stayed on the outside. That suited us fine because it meant we could do virtually whatever we wanted.

Because we were political prisoners, Long Kesh was run as a training school for Terrorists! On parade we even wore our uniforms. Each morning we all gathered in the exercise yard, and we had to do parade drill. After breakfast we would have weapon training classes. Sounds incredible but it's the truth; we even had bomb making lessons! All our teachers were experienced in these matters. I learned more from them inside about terrorism than I did outside.

It was possible to see through the wire into the next compound, which was full of Republican prisoners. The authorities thought doing this would stop communication between other Loyalist compounds. They assumed because we were enemies we would not bother with each other. It didn't work. If we wanted a message passed down to another of the Protestant compounds we would shout over to the Republicans and then throw the message attached to a half pound block of margarine (prison ration) over to them, and they would then in turn throw it over to the next compound. You could stand and watch to make sure they passed it on. They always did. It was an unspoken rule: you did not interfere with any of these notes, you simply passed them on. So each group could keep in touch with their own kind in any of the other compounds.

Once or twice some of our guys would mimic their voice and shout out an order.

It was quite odd really, seeing the enemy at such close range. They did parade ground drill just like us. The only difference was they shouted out their orders in the Gaelic language. After watching their parade drill for a while, we soon picked up what the order was being given. Once or twice some of our guys would mimic their voice and shout out an order and watch as they all turned in response. Although we thought it funny, we were told by our own commander not to do it anymore.

We looked forward to the weekends; they were more slack – we didn't parade or have classes. On Saturday nights we had a sing-a-long and made home brew to drink. The home brew was more like rocket fuel than a drink. It was made of a mixture of fruit and petrol from our cigarette lighters. Sometimes we threw in brass and copper polish to add to the taste. I was always amazed how the colour and taste were never the same. It made guys crazy, doing all kinds of mad things. We had no idea how bad these drunken escapades would get or what they would eventually lead to.

I was walking around the compound one day, and when I looked across into compound 10 – the Republican compound next to us. I saw something unusual. There was a Republican walking around with huge bandages covering both his hands, and his face was burned as well. I just stared at him, he looked a mess. I found out a few days later that he had been blown up by his own bomb. While he was planting it, it exploded prematurely and blew his hands off. He was badly injured. He was the enemy so we had no sympathy for him. The next time I saw him, I was walking around with a few other guys. When he passed by us, one of the guys shouted over to him through the wire making a derogative comment about his condition. Again we all laughed. He was given a nickname that day by which he became known to all the Loyalists. I had no idea then I would meet this same man, twenty-five years later, and he would embrace me as a brother! He also would come to know the grace of God in his own life, and like me, Michael

I had no idea then I would meet this same man, twenty-five years later, and he would embrace me as a brother!

would become a Minister of the Gospel!

Another interesting event that broke the monotony happened one evening. It was near time for lock-up, I was walking around the perimeter wire, and a Republican shouted over to me, "Do you want to see something funny? Wait till you see what happens next," so I stopped to see what he was up to. I didn't have long to wait; when the screw walked past with his guard-dog, the guy shouted to him. He told the screw, "I shouldn't be here," the screw laughed but the guy carried on to explain why. He had actually come up to visit his brother, and his brother walked out in his place. The screw didn't know what to do next; he questioned him for another few minutes and then reported the whole thing through his radio to the prison control. It turned out to be true; his brother was on remand for murder, and earlier that day during their visit they exchanged clothes and managed to swap places. Their plan had worked a treat!

It was very near Christmas and the courts would stop soon. So I knew it would be early in the new year (1974) before my trial would come to court. I just tried to settle down and wait. Let the time pass.

One of my saddest experiences of prison was that of Christmas 1973. We had drunk home brew all day. Later on in the evening my friend Geordie and I were on top of my bed watching television. He slept in the hut next door and it was near time for lock up. He said to me, "I'm away, I'll see you in the morning." But it wasn't to be. Later on that same night, there was a lot of commotion from the hut next door where Geordie slept. Someone gave a scream and a few minutes later everything went strangely quiet. The following morning, we were wakened by the sound of the sirens going off. Apparently when the screws came to unlock the hut doors, they found a battered dead body lying in a pool of blood.

It was that of my friend Geordie! We were locked up for two weeks while the authorities tried to solve the murder. I never really found out the reason why it happened, if there was any. The only comment made was, "It was the home brew to blame." Like most prison murders no one was ever charged for it. When we finally were unlocked, we all went into the hut next door.

I shall never forget the sick feeling I had when I saw the pool of congealed blood. We didn't expect to see that. The authorities just left it the way they had found it. It hadn't been touched, never mind cleaned up. I had seen plenty of blood in my time; the scars on my arms and hands are vivid reminders that violence played a big part in my life, but this was altogether different. I was sickened by what I saw. Everyone just stared at the large dark red stain of blood in the middle of the floor. I don't think anyone spoke; if they did, I wasn't aware of it. No one wanted to go near it, never mind clean it. After a few minutes I told them I would wash it off. After all, he had been one of my mates. Geordie's murder had a profound affect on a lot of people.

Many of the guys, including me, lost the desire for the home brew after that.

To end on a happier note, one of my happiest memories of that period was of a particular prison visit at that time. It was from my mother and the girl next door; her name was Sharon. I always thought she was beautiful – I remember the first time I saw her. Her family had not long moved from Belfast. One day I was walking up the garden path which we shared. She was standing with her mum at the front door, talking to my mum. It made my day when I found out she was our new neighbour! When I joined the Tartan gang, she sewed the tartan on my denim jacket for me. I tried once to get a kiss from her when she was in our house. I was seventeen; she was only fourteen at the time. I tried to grab her but she pulled away and ran out the back door and into her own house. I hadn't much skills in chatting girls up, so no doubt I went about it the wrong way. I took her running away as a sign that she wasn't interested in me as a boyfriend and so I gave up chasing her.

I took her running away as a sign that she wasn't interested in me as a boyfriend and so I gave up chasing her.

She was the girl who visited me when I was in jail for the first time, and as God would have it, she would be the woman who would be waiting for me at the gate when I would leave jail for the last time – ten years later. But a lot of things would happen to both of us before we would be joined together as husband and wife.

I want to share part of her story here.

THE BRUISED REED SYMBOLISES MY LIFE

I was born at home in a bungalow in Belfast situated on the shores of Belfast Lough. When I was three we moved to a big house in Alexander Park Avenue. Some of my fondest memories are from our family living there. I had an older brother Billy, who was three years older than me. I have vivid memories of my dad coming home from work. I knew when he would be due home from work. I would watch out the window or wait at the door, and once I got a glimpse of him I would charge down the avenue and he would stoop down and scoop me up in his arms. I thought we were a happy family, but all of that was to change quite suddenly.

One day when I was six, I was kept back from school but my brother Billy was sent to school alone. I didn't understand why. All I remember was my mother telling me she was taking me somewhere else. We went to a neighbour's house and picked up some suitcases that were already packed. Then we went to 'the cinema' – back then we called it going to 'the pictures'. I guess this was to fill the time. Later that afternoon my mum met up with this man and he carried our cases. We all went to England on the big boat that evening.

Meanwhile Billy came home from school. Billy had a house key to let himself in – to an empty house. He didn't know where we were. Usually my dad would be home from work around 5 o'clock, but on this particular day, he stayed to do overtime at work and didn't get home until 8 o' clock. Billy was frightened when it began to get dark. He was in the house alone so he went outside and sat on the front step and waited for Dad to come home. That's where Dad found him. Dad asked, "Where's Mum and Sharon?" Of course, Billy didn't know, but he said there was a note in the kitchen. It read, *"Sharon's with me. Dinner's in the oven."* That was all. As the evening wore on Dad got very alarmed. He left Billy at my granny's and went to search for Mum and me. He thought something had happened to us. He knew nothing of what was going on. No one seemed to know anything of our whereabouts.

A week later Mum and me arrived back but we didn't go home as I expected to. Instead we went back to my granny's house. That evening my dad arrived, but Mum didn't want to speak to him and my grandmother refused to let him see us. "Come back tomorrow," she said and closed the door on his face. He was anxious; I could hear him pleading at the door. I couldn't understand all what was going on. All I knew was that I wanted to see my daddy and go home and see my brother Billy. I really had missed them so much! It didn't happen. I was now living in my granny's. I was sent to a new school the following day.

A week later my dad came to meet me coming home from school. I ran and jumped into his arms. He gave me a big hug and I was kissing his face. I told him I had really missed him and Billy. We went back to my granny's house and Dad told her he was taking me home. He told me to go in and to grab some of my stuff. I didn't know what he meant by that; I just grabbed my new skates that this other man had bought me as a present whilst we were in England. I didn't want to leave them behind – I wanted to take them with me.

It was great to be back home with my dad and Billy – but mummy wasn't there. Billy was excited to see me. We hadn't seen each other for a few weeks, but to us it seemed like a year!

My dad was trying to keep us together as a family and hold down a job. (He worked as a crane driver). But all of this proved to be too much for him, trying to keep two school children and be in work for 8 o'clock. He tried to make it work, but eventually I was sent back to live with my mum.

My first day home, I wasn't really at ease around this man we had been to England with. My mum saw this and then started shouting at me and called me all kinds of names. She said how evil I was, that I was happy to take the present from him. It would take a while before I could begin to understand what was going on, but then I was completely puzzled as to what it was I had actually done to be punished for.

This was to be the scene for the next ten years, back and forth, from one to the other. From one house to another. Eventually the situation began to dawn on me, I began to realise who this other man was; he was the reason for my dad's loneliness and pain!

When this truth began to dawn on me – I was overwhelmed with such condemnation, I was sick in my stomach. I felt such a traitor – the guilt was overwhelming; there was I sitting on this man's knee and accepting presents from him. I hated myself for betraying my dad whom I said I loved, yet I did these terrible things to him. I saw myself as a terrible person. I began to hate myself, I could barely look at my dad; it seemed all I could see was his pain etched all over his face – as if this wasn't enough for him to suffer. I felt I had caused him more pain because of what I did. The emotions that rose up in me began to tear me apart inside. I just didn't know how to cope.

When I was 11, one day I went to visit my mum. But she wasn't in, just this other man. He told me I now had a baby sister (she was actually born on my dad's birthday!) I thought this was fantastic and couldn't wait to tell Dad the news; he would be over the moon! Of course, I was just a child, still too young to understand all the issues.

At 14, I had to go stay with my mum again. At this time she was living in Rathcoole and her next door neighbours were a family called the 'Hamiltons'. And then it happened! One day I was looking out the front window and I saw this boy walking up our street. My heart skipped a beat as I looked at him; he was the most handsome boy I'd ever seen. To my delight he turned and walked up our garden path; he was the boy next door! I fell in love immediately. It really was love at first sight! But as a young girl of fourteen I couldn't cope with love. I got to know all his sisters, before I got to know him. On one occasion, I was in town with one of David's older sisters, Lynn.

She decided to get a tattoo on her arm of her boyfriend's name. While we were in the studio, I asked the tattooist if I could have a name put on my arm. He asked how old I was; I actually looked much younger. But I told him the truth; I was only fourteen. He said I was too young to have it done. Outside Lynn held her arm

My heart skipped a beat as I looked at him; he was the most handsome boy I'd ever seen.

out for me to see the finished job and asked me what I thought of her tattoo. She asked me what was it I had wanted tattooed on mine. I told her, "I wanted to have your David's name put on my arm!"

David was a skinhead, a gang member of the notorious KAI who wore red tartan scarves. I volunteered to sew tartan unto his denim wrangler jacket. When he was 17 he got involved with the paramilitaries and was sent to prison. I went to visit him with his mum. I hadn't seen him for quite a while, but when I did, it was just like the first day I saw him; again my heart just fluttered whenever I was around him. I couldn't speak and I just sat and smiled the whole time of the visit.

I decided the best thing to do was for us to get married and get a place of our own.

After a while I went back to live with my dad again. On one occasion I went out with a boy, I was incredibly naïve. I hadn't started to date boys yet, this was first. It was a disaster – I was only sixteen when I ended up getting pregnant. I tried to tell my mum, but she just said, "I can't talk now I have to go, or I will be late for bingo," and off she went – that was it. I was all screwed up. I thought, I must love this boy if I let him do this to me. I decided the best thing to do was for us to get married and get a place of our own. My parents consented, and we got married and the baby was born just before my 17th birthday. The marriage was crazy from day one. He was a control freak. I wasn't allowed to speak to anyone and had to account for my movements. Wherever I went he would time me, he was so insecure. After just a few months we split up. When my baby, Louise, was four months old I decided I wanted to have her christened. I went along to the local church and got it all arranged. I decided as the father he had a right to come if he wanted to. I went to see him and give him the invitation. As we were standing talking at the door, I looked at him and suddenly blurted out, "I don't know why I married you, for I have always loved David Hamilton."

Needless to say, he never made an appearance at the christening. When the baby was 8 months old we got back together again. I thought for the child's sake we should make a go of it and try to make our marriage work. We moved into my dad's flat thinking that might help the situation. In fact, it made things worse between us. He became very jealous even of my dad, because he said I showed my dad more attention than I did him. Two months later my dad had a heart attack and died a few days later. My husband was so nonchalant; he couldn't show any support or sympathy for me even then and I was heartbroken. It was then I realized my marriage was never going to work out either; it was over. We split up, this time for good.

My life was a complete mess. I was so alone. Really I wanted to die, but because I had this little person depending on me I had to go on. I know had I not had this child I would have committed suicide. She was the reason I couldn't. Looking back now I realize God used my baby to keep me alive. (*Continued later*)

Chapter Six

DAVEY THE PRISONER

It was early in the new year. I was shocked to hear my name called, "Hamilton, pack your bags!" I couldn't believe what the screw said! I was to pack my bags. I must be getting released. It wasn't to be – I was being moved into YPs, (another part of the prison for sentenced Young Prisoners.) I had been sentenced in my absence and I had to pay a fine. I couldn't recall any of this, but I was informed I had to serve a three-month sentence. I was a sentenced prisoner! I was taken to reception and stripped and given a prison uniform to put on. The worst part of all of this for me was when I realised I had to walk back past Compound 9 – where I had just come from on my way to compound 15. I think I prayed then asking God to make sure they were all locked up. I dreaded anyone seeing me in this prison garb, but sure enough someone spotted me and shouted to everybody else. In seconds about forty guys were all at the wire shouting, pointing and laughing at me. I was humiliated! I just had to look away and hide by beetroot face. I hastened my steps to get pass out of range!

I thought things couldn't get any worse, but I was in for another nasty surprise. I walked into Compound 15. It was the same layout as the other compounds: consisting of 4 billets, and an ablution hut. I went first into the screw's office, received a lecture and was then placed in a hut. I lifted all my garb. Earlier, I had been given two blankets, two sheets, a pillow sheet and a pillow, socks and a mug, with a bar of soap and a toothbrush in reception.

As I left the office, just outside I met another YP – (Young Prisoner) as they were called. Every prisoner here was under the age of 18. He stopped and stared at me as if he recognised me. I stared back at him too, thinking to myself, I know him from somewhere. Simultaneously we both realized where we had met before. I had fought this guy on the street about a year before in a gang fight in the centre of Belfast. He was a Catholic gang member. He immediately said to me, "Remember this?" and he pointed to the scar on his forehead; I had hit him with a welder's hammer at the time. I remembered the incident clearly. Although he was covered in blood he didn't go down as I expected him to. Quite the opposite in fact. He immediately attacked me with a round of rapid culmination punches to my body and head. I backed off, trying to get a bit of space to gather what was happening. But he didn't let up; he continued his attack, pounding me mercilessly. I threw a few punches to no avail. He beat me till I crumbled to the ground. When some of my mates saw what was happening they came running to my rescue. It was only then he took off and got away. I didn't know who he was, but I found out later, he had a reputation of being a street fighter. His name was 'Wee Buck' and he was a hard case. He came from the Davis Flats area in Belfast.

He didn't let up; he continued his attack, pounding me mercilessly.

He just walked on. I thought, this is all I need right now, I got a Taig (slang word for Roman Catholic) I need to watch out for; he will be looking for a chance to get even. I will have to be extra cautious. I need to get myself a weapon real soon before this kicks off between us.

I was the new kid on the block here – I was alone. I only knew one guy and he was an enemy. Things are tough in a borstal situation like this. I knew what to expect, you will be picked on to find out your pecking order and where you fit in as it were. As a gang member, there is safety in numbers. The gang will always support you. Bullying is the norm here especially if you're alone. I had to wait it out and see if I could identify a Protestant gang who perhaps would accept me.

The first night is always rough in Borstal for everyone. I went into the hut I was allocated and someone pointed out a bed. Of course, it was the worst bed in the place! Half the springs were missing. I made up my bed; bed packs were the norm. I just lay down on top of the bed, looking around. Many of them were looking back at me too. I was happy about one thing that first night in the hut. The guy 'Wee Buck' was not sleeping in this particular hut. But I knew I would have to deal with him in the next few days. It doesn't take long to spot who's in charge of the hut, who's 'The Man.' I was surprised to find out I was not actually the only new kid on the block after all. There were three of us; this was our first night. About two hours after we were banged up, I could sense something was coming down, the atmosphere was changing, guys were looking around, or towards this guy who obviously was the one who would give the order. Sure enough only a minute later he walked into the middle of the hut and addressed us new guys, looking at each of us in turn. We were informed he was the boss of this hut – what he said went, or there would be trouble. Not that I was surprised as he had been ordering a few weak guys around earlier, to do this, do that for him. It was really a show for us new guys but he honestly did look that hard to me and he had all these cronies around him. As he was talking to us, I was listening and looking around me at the same time. All the other guys around the hut started to remove their pillow cases; I saw guys putting boots inside them or books and tying them in a knot, and before wrapping them around their hands they all stood at the end of their beds.

The main guy spoke. "First night here, you have to run the gauntlet, from one end to the other. Don't stop until you reach and touch the other wall. If you fall down make sure you get up right away or they will continue to beat you and the beating continues until you touch that wall." He pointed to the wall opposite the doorway.

The other two new guys looked at each other, horrified! "Who wants to go first?" he shouted. "I will," I said, jumping off the bed. I made my way down to the doorway. It's not that I was the bravest, I knew it had to be done. My thinking was, If I go first, I'll have it over me quicker! If I wait and watch the other two first, it's just enduring the whole thing. All eyes were on me now, "Whenever you're ready!" he shouted. I took a few deep breaths and made a dash. The blows were fast and furious, I was trying to protect my face and at the same time see what direction I was heading. Within seconds I felt a tremendous blow to my face and the next thing I saw again

"Who wants to go first?" he shouted. "I will," I said jumping off the bed.

when I opened my eyes was my own blood filling my hands. All the while these blows were raining down on my head, back and arms. I had to force myself into this wall of bombardment in front of me. Some of these guys were loving this; they were screaming with delight – especially when they saw the blood. They were trying to force me to stop advancing. I knew if I stopped I would never get a chance to start again, plus there was the danger of going down. Some of the blows were trying to do that very thing, I was in no doubt what the outcome would be if I stumbled and went down; some of these guys would continue to beat me until I was unconscious.

No sooner had it started that it came to an end, I don't think it lasted more than a couple of minutes. I got to touch the other wall. I stood upright and took a few gulps of air as I looked around at them all. I started to laugh, they laughed too. A guy handed me a toilet roll and said "Here, wipe your face," I smiled at him, "Thanks mate".

I was alright after a few minutes; all the cuts and bruises were only superficial. From past experience I knew my nose wasn't broke, just sore. "Who's next?" the main guy called out.

All eyes turned to see, one of the new guys blurt out "No way are you doing that to me! I refuse to do it – if you come near me I'll call the screws." Everyone laughed at this. Obviously, he didn't know the score; once locked up the screws don't come back to open the doors, they remain shut until 7am the next morning.

"If you don't then it will be a lot worse, believe me." "It will be twice as bad for you," he answered, "I don't care, I am not doing that." Not another word was said. They looked at the other guy who really didn't know what to do, he was literally shaken. He then made his way to the doorway, touched the wall behind himself and began to prepare himself to take the charge.

"Here you can beat him now," a guy said to me and handed his pillow case toward me. I refused, making the excuse that I didn't want my nose to start bleeding again. The whole thing was repeated, after a few minutes it was over, I don't think he was seriously hurt by the beating. All eyes turned to the other guy; he made no move to get off the bed; he didn't speak. He just sat shaking his head.

Guys started to untie their pillow cases and dismantle their bed-packs to make up their beds for the night. As the night wore on, still not a word was said to the other new guy. I thought to myself, this thing is not over yet. The screw came around and turned the lights off at 11 o'clock, the lights were operated from outside the front doors. After a few moments your eyes adjusted to the light that remained in the hut. After another few minutes we heard the screws leaving the compound and locking the main gates. They would not be back until early morning. Eventually I managed to fall asleep. I don't know how long I was sleeping for before I was awakened by a terrifying scream. I turned and looked down the length of the hut: four or five guys were around the new guy's bed. He was pinned down by the blue towel with guys on each side of the bed making sure he couldn't move. It was a frightening scene; each of these guys were hooded with a white pillow case. The scariest part of all was another hooded guy sitting astride this poor guy, and a gag had been pushed into the victim's mouth. The guy on top of him slowly and deliberately ran a razor blade across his face, this he did several times. He climbed off him and laughed.

The poor guy was then released, he leaned over the bed and picked up a towel from the floor and sunk his face into it. He laid and cried into this towel the rest of the night. The next morning, he ran screaming out the doors as soon as the screws opened our hut. He was taken down to the prison hospital compound. The PO came in and asked what had happened to him. I don't think he was really expecting an answer. Someone said, "He tried shaving in the dark."

Someone said, "He tried shaving in the dark."

All the guys burst out laughing. As usual, in jail when these things happen, no one has seen anything, they all were fast asleep. No one was ever charged for this incident. So that was my first night in Compound 15.

The next morning after I made my bed pack up and got washed I made my way into the canteen, there were around 70-80 guys there. They all stared at the two new guys – some of the guys from our hut were telling them the story of last night's event. I joined the line and lifted a tray for my breakfast. I was in front of the other new guy, he was letting me take the lead. I got a couple of rounds of toast and a hard-boiled egg. I saw an empty table so I made my way to it. 'Stew' followed me (I found later that was the other new guy's name). We just sat together. I saw 'Wee Buck' a few tables away, he looked over a few times at me, but I made sure I didn't make eye contact with him. Most of the guys were in cliques, all from different parts of the country. I sat looking around at the rest of these guys, then I spotted a face I knew. It was an old Catholic friend I had known from way back. Believe it or not, he was actually one of the guys who threw me into the river a few years ago. He had moved from Rathcoole into a Catholic area in Belfast. He acted as if he didn't know me; he didn't want any of his Republican friends to think he had any Protestant friends. By the way he was getting on it was best for me not to even speak to him. After breakfast we were put on a work party, I found myself taking trolleys laden with food from the kitchen to the various compounds. To my relief I was not allowed to go near Compound 9, in case I should be smuggling or carrying messages from any of the other compounds. I was so relieved with this news as I had been embarrassed enough the day before having to walk past them all. I had no desire to go near the place. The work parties were made up of everybody, regardless of religion. Again I was glad to see 'Wee Buck' was put somewhere else to work. This was the easiest part of the day. It was in the evening, when we are all out on recreation, as someone rightly said, that's when prison starts.

It was in the evening, when we are all out on recreation, that's when prison starts.

After the work details were all back, we were banged up before having our tea. When we were released again all the guys charge towards the canteen, to get as far up the food chain as possible. Again those who were not involved or recognised as a gang member had to wait until others had been fed before they could join the line. I deliberately took my time before taking a place in the queue. Other guys didn't queue at all, they just walked to the front and got served immediately. I noticed 'Wee Buck' was one of them. As we shuffled forward I looked to see what was being served up: it was sausages, beans, and chips. You were allowed as much bread as you wanted. As I approached the serving hatch the server looked at me, and as he tilted some of the beans back into the Dixie, I never said anything. I walked to the next guy who was dishing out the sausages – on some of the guys' trays he put only one, on other trays he put three. We were meant to have two each. Those who got one didn't say anything.

To be honest this was typical of Borstal bullying treatment; the bullying that goes on is unbelievable. It just has to be seen first-hand to be believed. I have seen guys having to perform sexual acts on other guys while in the shower blocks. They were forced to do these things or face dire consequences. Or at night they would put someone inside a locker and keep them locked in it for three or four hours before allowing them to come out.

When it came to my turn in the queue, the server looked at me and dropped a sausage back down again into the Dixie can. I received a single sausage. I now had a problem to deal with, I stopped and looked at him. "Move along there," someone shouted, "you're holding up the queue." I was a bit flustered so I just moved on. Stew who was behind me, got one sausage as well. When everyone had been served, the fat guy who was the server walked across to the table where he sat, with a gang of guys from his own area, which happened to be a place in Belfast. He dished out the extra sausages around the table. I was giving him the evil eye in disgust, he smiled over to where I sat, and a few of his cronies turned to look across at our table. I was glad he knew I was not very happy. So I thought I have to do something about this guy. Stew mentioned it later to me, and I said he won't get away with it next time: "I love sausages too much, I want extra."

I had to wait a whole week before it was sausage time again. I had made up my mind; I wanted my fair share. Sure enough, when he saw me coming, he dropped a sausage off the fork and set the one on my plate. I said to him, "Set the other one on too, fatso." He looked at me, I didn't move, so again someone shouted, "What's the hold up?"

"I'm waiting for my sausages," I said.

He got flustered, stabbed another sausage and tossed it to my tray. "I'll sort you out later," he hissed at me. "I'll see you too." Stew still got only one sausage. After we all were served "Fat Mat" as he was called by everybody, went over to the table and spoke a couple of sentences, while sharing out the extra food amongst them. Next thing all of them turned around and they just stared at me. I just smiled and enjoyed my two sausages. Stew said to me in a whisper, "You're for it now Davey!" Before we had finished our tea, one of them came over to me and said, "'Fat Mat' wants to see you in the ablutions after lock up."

"I'll be there," I said. "So will we," he said pointing to the rest of them around the table. He walked back to the table and told 'Fat Mat' it was arranged.

It looked like the odds were stacked against me, seven to one. Stew said, "I can't help you mate, I'm not a fighter." I told him not to worry himself, I wasn't expecting anyone else to get involved in my troubles.

What happened next was a real shock to me, and everyone else there too. 'Wee Buck' got up and walked over and set down at our table opposite me. He looked me in the face and said, "Are you happy to fight that fat ass alone?"

"No problem," I answered.

"Then I'll back you, Davey." Before I could say a word in reply, he then turned around and said to them all, "I'll second Davey, anyone who wants to join in, it's fine by me."

That's when I found out 'Wee Buck' was feared by them all: the look on their faces said it all. With that he got up and walked away to his own table and sat down again. He had been watching the whole thing. I could not believe what had just happened. Why is he backing me? I was the one who hit him with a hammer.

Half an hour later, someone nodded to me. It was time to go out to the ablutions. 'Fat Mat' got up as well. None of his gang moved. The doorway of the ablutions hut was very narrow and you had to step up to enter through it. 'Fat Mat' made his move while I was still stepping in. I expected something like this from him. I blocked his kick and stood upright. He then lowered his head and made a lunge at me. I hit him with a massive uppercut; he seemed to rise up off the ground. I followed *'Fat Mat' got up as well. None of his gang moved.* through with several body punches as he fell back against the wall. I then hit him twice on the face and he fell to the ground, shouting, "OK you win, you win." I continued to give him

71

a few kicks before I turned and walked outside, a few of his mates were standing round. As I looked at them, they looked down, they didn't want to know, they were only watching to see the outcome. 'Wee Buck' smiled and said, "What kept you so long in there, were you at the toilet too?" I just laughed. The next week, 'Fat Mat' was nicer to me. He put two sausages on my tray. I didn't move, I give him a dirty look, he took the hint and dropped me an extra sausage. I just smiled at him. Stew still only got the one. So I gave him the extra one I had after we sat down.

I was puzzled about 'Wee Buck' and a week later I asked him why he helped me. "I hate bullies," he said.

"But what about our fight remember? I beat you with a hammer."

"Na," he said. "You hit me with a hammer, if I remember right, but I think it was I that won that fight." We both had a good laugh.

After that we became the best of mates. We developed a friendship that lasted for years. Years later, he invited me to his wedding which was up the Falls Road in Belfast. I said to him at that time, "Are you mad?" He laughed and said, "You're safe with me." When I got out of jail I used to go into the pub where he drank. Some of my own mates thought I had a death wish walking into a Republican bar in the middle of Castle Street but I knew as a friend of 'Wee Buck's' I was safe.

I had almost served my three-month sentence. I knew it would be finished in a day or two. I had dared hope there might be a possibility I would be released and get home. Sure enough I was called, "Hamilton time served." Some of the guys cheered, those whom I had got to know. The 'old' Catholic friend from the past actually spoke to me that day too. Later on he came over and wished me all the best. I said thanks, but he went on to say, "If I see you outside, Davey, you're dead."

"Maybe I'll see you first," I answered back.

The screw escorted me down to the reception area. I was given back my own clothes to wear. I was quite excited about the prospect of getting released. Eventually I was allowed to pass through the turn style into the car park; that was as far as I got. I walked a little further. It was then I saw two men in plain clothes start to walk towards me. I knew immediately they were police. "You're under arrest," one of them said. I was escorted back into reception, went through the whole hassle once again – I was brought back down to Compound 9 once more.

Chapter Seven

BACK ON THE STREETS

Eventually I was moved back up to the Crumlin Road jail. So I knew my trial would be pretty soon. It was around this time I began to pray. (I had not prayed since I was a young boy.) Not that they were long prayers, mostly one liners like, "God get me out of here and I'll be good from now on" … I had learned about God at Sunday school; I believed God existed OK and thought if I make a deal with him he would help me beat this rap. So I began to pray every day when it would enter my mind.

Other days I prayed something like, "God I promise I'll start going back to church again if you just get me out!" I thought that was a good deal, if I prayed it once I must have prayed it a hundred times. When my trial came up eventually, the judge sentenced me to a five year stretch! I couldn't believe it! For an attempted armed robbery and stealing a few cars! To me it was no robbery; it was more of a joke! Only now it was far from being funny: who said praying helps? It didn't seem to help me! That night as I lay in my cell looking up at the ceiling, I thought, *five years! That's what happens when you pray!*

I was sick at the thought of having to serve a five year stretch. As I lay there looking up at the ceiling I noticed someone had written their name up in the corner of the wall. As I stared up at it I was shocked to see whose name it was. It was the name of my friend who had been murdered a few months before! I couldn't believe it, neither could I grumble; seeing his name actually stopped me feeling sorry for myself.

At least I was alive.

I didn't even bother to undress that night; I lay down on top of the bed. It was well into the early hours of the morning before I finally got to sleep. Next morning, it was the screw who woke me up as he banged up the door, i.e. locking it back to the wall. As I looked out at him he said, "Get ready for court, Hamilton."

"Not me," I shouted back.

"Listen Hamilton, I've orders to get you over to the court, so get washed right now; you are going, like it or not."

The High Court in Northern Ireland is only across the road from the prison in Belfast. In fact, you do not even have to leave the prison to go to court. The two buildings are connected by an underground tunnel that runs beneath the main road. Walking through the tunnel was unpleasant, to say the least. It was very hot and clammy. From the moment you begin the six-minute walk across you are aware of the lack of air down there. There are huge water pipes that run the length of the tunnel along one side. They are caged off, in case someone should get burnt accidentally.

After climbing up the steps at the other end I passed through the door, and suddenly found myself standing in the dock of a courtroom with a prison officer on each side of me. I was amazed to find the place was empty apart from the two prison officers and myself.

I did not really know what to expect in court; as far as I was aware all four of my charges where dealt with the day before. I was worried in case I got more time added on to my existing five years. As I stood there in the dock with all kinds of thoughts racing through my mind, a door across the room opened and I saw a familiar face; it was my barrister. *At last I'll get some answers, he will know what this is all about,* or so I thought. "What are the charges against me today?" I asked. I could not believe it when he turned his hands up and shrugged his shoulders, saying he did not know either! Like me, he also had been strangely summoned to the courtroom that morning as well. I was really discouraged then. How could my lawyer provide a defence for me if he didn't even know what charges were being brought? Things looked bad! I began to sweat! Before I got a chance to challenge him, two officers came through from the judge's chamber.

Things looked bad! I began to sweat!

"Everyone please stand," the bailiff bellowed as the judge entered the courtroom. We then took our seats again. I began to study the judge, hoping he was in a good mood today. He looked very solemn sitting there with all his long robes on and the traditional white wig perched on his head. It's amazing what enters your mind at times. I was trying to figure out what kept his spectacles on the end of his nose. Occasionally he would lower his head to peep over the rim at me – I was waiting for them to fall off. It's a good thing they did not, or I would have gone into a fit of laughter and ended up with more time for contempt of court.

I had to stand up the whole time while the judge was speaking to me. To be perfectly honest, I was not really paying much attention to the lecture he was giving me. Occasionally I nodded my head towards him to give the impression that I was paying attention. But when I heard him say that he had decided to change my sentence to a recorded sentence, (a recorded sentence is when the offender is released and his custodial sentence is only implemented if he re-offends) I could not believe my ears! As I was looking around in amazement, I saw my mother sitting in the public gallery. I gave her a huge smile and the thumbs up sign, I was going home! A free man! Perhaps there was something in this prayer business after all.

The judge went on to say he did not want to see my face ever again.

The judge went on to say he did not want to see my face ever again. Sad to say we were to meet again, not that long after. Not only that, but he would remember my face as well!

A few months later, I was sitting in a restaurant along with an old girlfriend (I started to date her again when I came home from prison) and another couple. Although we had been drinking all evening I could not seem to get drunk. I was aware that the place where we were eating was not a safe place for any Protestant to be because it was adjacent to a strong Republican neighbourhood. I was glad when we paid the bill and headed toward the door.

As we left the restaurant I saw two men standing a few yards away, one of them was bent over appearing to be sick, the other man had his arm across his friend's back. I thought it was strange because the man standing up never took his eyes off me the whole time as we were passing by.

All at once the man who was bent over straightened up and pulled a gun from under his jacket! I shouted to my friends, "Run, he has a gun." I did not know which way to run. In front of me across the road was an open field; it was pitch black over there. I decided to make a dash there, but suddenly stopped turned around and ran back into the restaurant! I was puzzled with my own behaviour; it seemed silly to run back into the restaurant. Inside the door I shouted a warning. No one moved: they all just sat and stared at me. I heard the door being kicked open and looked around to see one of the gunmen coming in. I began to run again, knocking tables over as I made my way through the kitchen. I could see the startled faces of the Chinese cooks, who knew by my face that something was seriously wrong. I just managed to get the back door open when I heard the gunman behind me run into the kitchen. I jumped on to a pile of rubbish bins and leaped on to the top of the wall, knowing the gunman was not far behind me. Just as I dropped down into the alley I heard the large crack of two shots. As soon as my feet touched the ground I was away. It was not safe yet; these guys knew the area as well as I did, if not better. I ran up onto the railway tracks, which ran along by the beach. I cursed the moon. It was shining bright, too bright. *What a beautiful night to be murdered.*

I was silhouetted against the night sky, thanks to the moon! Suddenly the deadly silence was shattered by the sound of more gunfire. I immediately threw myself down to the ground for cover behind the railway lines. Other shots followed, but they were different from the others, which made me think something else was happening now. The next thing I heard was the sirens of the security forces piercing the night air as they arrived on the scene. It was only then that I knew it was safe to return to the restaurant. As I was walking back, I was worried about how my girl and my two friends had fared. As I got back, the place was swarming with security forces. It seemed the police saw one of the gunmen and started to give chase, but they ran into the field and were able to escape being captured. I found out later they had knocked my girl to the ground, as they started to chase after me. Although shaken up both she and my friends were safe and sound. Their faces said it all. They had heard the shots and were afraid I was lying dead or seriously wounded somewhere. The police officer came over to us and asked me how did I know to turn back. He went on to tell me there had been a gunman waiting across the road in the field. My attackers had expected me to run there for cover because it was the most obvious place to go. For no apparent reason I had turned back again to the restaurant.

Had I continued running I surely would have been killed at point-blank range! Everyone said I was extremely lucky, I had narrowly escaped death. But I just laughed. I was too smart for them boys! It would be years before I would know the truth that it was God who made me turn and run in the other direction. It was God who spared my life. But for the time being, I carried on with my usual crazy lifestyle. Nothing changed apart from one thing; I made sure I avoided that particular restaurant. Since then, I have never been comfortable sitting with my back to the door in any restaurant.

My dad sincerely wanted me to work hard and stay out of trouble and prison. Although only out of prison that Friday morning, before taking me home he drove me up to the factory where I had been serving my apprenticeship as a welder before going to prison. The manager kindly gave me my job back, so the following Monday I was back at work! I didn't share my dad's enthusiasm about working but he thought my job would keep me out of paramilitary organisations. Sadly it didn't work. I wasn't out that long, before I joined the organisation again – in fact it was the following night.

It was more from peer influence than peer pressure from my mates that I got back involved in the paramilitaries. Almost everyone my age was a member of one the terrorist groups or another. If you were not involved, you were a 'nobody' and had no protection from any of the gang members that roamed the neighbourhoods. I had already decided to join another group called the Ulster Volunteer Force. Because the police were watching both the gang members and *The UVF was more militant and violent against the IRA.* paramilitaries in our area, obviously we were all well known to them. I decided to join a paramilitary unit outside my neighbourhood. It was a team from the Shore Road, part of the Tiger Bay area, a famous area in Belfast known for its many gun battles. The UVF was more militant and violent against the IRA; they were also very secretive. I was intrigued by them. The only way to join the UVF was by invitation from one of its present members. I had made it known around the jail that I wanted to join. I didn't have long to wait before two strangers came to my home and asked if I wanted to be part of their group. I said yes. They gave me a week to think it over because they told me – *once you're in the UVF, you're in for life.*

A week later the men showed up at my house again. When I told them I definitely wanted to join they told me to go to a bar nearby. I remember walking through the doorway into the public bar, I didn't know what to expect. It was dimly lit and the smell of stale alcohol hung heavy in the air. Only a few of the old regulars were to be seen, huddled together in the corner. Above their heads a television blared away, forcing them to shout to be heard. None of them had the wit to turn the thing down or off.

"This is your last chance to say no. After this there can be no turning back."

I nodded to the barman who was busy drying beer glasses behind the counter. He nodded toward the other door, telling me where I was to go. I entered the door and a man stepped in front of me and put his finger on my chest. "Are you sure you want to do this?" he asked. "This is your last chance to say no. After this there can be no turning back."

"Yes, I want to," I replied. "This is a cause worth dying for!"

That afternoon I took the oath of loyalty and became a member of the Ulster Volunteer Force. As I left the pub I thought to myself, "Only God knows what the future holds for me." All I was sure of was that things would never be the same from that day on.

Shortly after I had joined we planned a bank robbery. I

was annoyed because they planned the heist for Thursday morning. That was the day I had to pick up my pay cheque so I couldn't take part in the robbery. When I came home from work that night my mate's wife was crying. She told me her husband had not come home. We watched the local television news and discovered four men, one of them her husband, had been arrested during a bank robbery earlier that day. Even though my best friend was in jail, it did nothing to deter me, I still continued on.

My girlfriend became pregnant and we decided to get married. She knew that I was involved in the UVF. She pleaded with me to try to find a way to get out and to keep her quiet I promised I would. But I lied. Our son was born six months after we were married. I went up to see my new-born son on the night he was born. I wasn't all that keen to visit the hospital, situated in a Republican area in Belfast – not a safe place for any Protestant to walk through. I was wearing my good suit (my wedding suit, kept for weddings and funerals.) I also had a bunch of flowers with me and something else. I knew I had to walk through an army check point, but decided to take the risk anyway. Passing through the barrier I raised my arms up to allow the soldier to frisk me. I was watching his face, and saw his expression change when he felt something down the back of my trousers. "What's this for?" the soldier asked, pulling a large kitchen knife out from under my coat. I simply told him the truth: being a Protestant it was likely I would be attacked by Catholics before I reached the hospital. I needed the knife for my own protection.

He stared into my face and after a few tense moments he handed me the flowers back, looked at the knife again, before handing it back to me as well. I breathed a sigh of relief! For a moment I had thought, *Crumlin Road, here I come.*

With a big smile I said thanks and walked away, at a fast trot down the street. Before turning the corner, I chanced a look back and saw that the soldier was still watching me. I hoped he hadn't changed his mind.

My mum had hoped with the birth of my child I would change my ways but it didn't happen. I was still as mad; there were times I did things on the spur of the moment. Once I was out walking with my wife and pushing my child in a pram. We met a large number of young gang members who were not old enough to join the ranks of the paramilitary group. I asked them what they were up to and one of them told me they planned to stone a bus in retaliation for police harassment earlier. I told them to wait and that I would hi-jack a bus for them to burn. I turned to my wife and said "I'll see you later."

Before she could answer, I had run off with them. Before she could answer, I had run off with them. I told them to hide when I saw a bus coming. The plan was I would board the bus and order everyone off, except the driver, who could drive the bus for us. When the bus stopped, I gave the signal and they all came out from hiding and boarded the bus. We drove it up into Rathcoole and set it across the main road and torched it. I left them to it and went back up to meet my wife at the shops again as if nothing had happened. I didn't care less about getting caught for it. My wife knew there was no point in bringing this up; she didn't even mention it; neither did I.

Over the next few months my wife eventually came to accept the situation. She knew I couldn't leave the organisation now even if I had wanted to. It had never entered my mind to try and get out; I believed it was a good cause and it was only right to fight for what I believed in. Looking back, I realised I had not really counted the cost nor did I know the price I would have to pay. I never once thought my marriage would break up, but it did. Sadly many marriages break up because a husband serves prison time.

Many people tried to talk to me about my crazy lifestyle, but I refused to listen to anyone. I never thought about the future, I just lived one day at a time. Besides, I didn't know anyone who had walked away from the UVF and lived long enough to boast about it. I continued to work at my old job but became more active in the paramilitary organisation. I even used my home to store weapons for the UVF. All I thought about was the Protestant cause, and fighting the Republican movement!

"This is a good day to rob a bank," I thought. I was aware of the sawn-off shotgun under my suit jacket; it was uncomfortable. I was hoping none of the other people standing at the bus stop would notice it. We had watched the bank for several weeks; our surveillance had paid off. Every morning the banker did the same thing at the same time. He opened the doors, turned off the alarm, and came back out into a hall to collect the mail. I thought the hall would be the best place to jump him. I planned to run into the hallway, shove a gun into his ribs and walk him back inside the bank. Other members of my team would then help me sack up all the money in the bank. I had rehearsed this over and over with the other members of the team, everyone knew what part they were to play. I was anxious for the guy to arrive. What was keeping him?

That morning as I stood waiting for the banker to arrive I was shocked when I heard someone call out, "Davey, are you not going to work today?" It was my boss! I couldn't believe it! He had pulled up in his car to offer me a ride to work! Here he was talking to me through the car window! It was difficult for me to bend over to answer him because of the gun under my coat. "I have to go somewhere but I will be in this afternoon," I whispered. I didn't want to talk to him so I said, "You're holding up traffic. I'll see you later." I was glad when he said, "OK, see you this afternoon." I breathed a sigh of relief and looked over at my mates standing across the street. They were dressed as painters, holding buckets and cans of paint. Only it wasn't paint inside the buckets and cans, it was guns!

I breathed a sigh of relief and looked over at my mates standing across the street.

They stared at me, waiting for me to start the operation. I looked back at the bank and thought I had missed my opportunity. The lights were on! While I had been talking to my boss the banker had arrived! A few moments later he went out into the hall. As he bent over to pick up the mail I ran up the steps, kicked him down to the floor and stuck the gun into his face. "Don't even breathe," I said. I grabbed him by the hair and shoved him into the foyer of the bank. We could not be seen from the outside because the windows were laminated with plastic half-way up. I signalled for my team members to come and join me just as we had planned. The banker then followed my instructions to lock the doors again.

We tried to open the night safe. Unfortunately, the keys to the safe were kept by another employee who had yet to arrive. We decided to wait for him! One by one other employees of the bank began to arrive. The manager and I let them in the front door and put them into a separate room out at the back where one of our gang held them at gun-point. A few minutes later something happened I wasn't expecting, I heard a noise at the window and when I looked up I saw the top of a ladder! I could not believe what I was seeing: someone was actually beginning to climb up it! This was not part of our plan; it was a real window cleaner! I grabbed the manager and told him to go outside and call the window cleaner to come into the bank. I warned the banker that if he tried anything else I would shoot him first. I was relieved when the window cleaner came in. I told him what was going on and put him in the next room with the other hostages.

By now we had been in the bank almost an hour. I knew our getaway driver would be beside himself. We finally got both safes open and filled briefcases with money. I let most of the team out though the front door again. The two of us who remained would leave by the back door with the money. As we walked toward the car an army patrol suddenly turned the corner and came directly towards us. I tried to act like a businessman so I spoke to the Army officer, "Not a bad day is it?" Obviously they were not suspicious of us and we walked by them to our waiting car.

Sometimes truth is stranger than fiction. What happened next is hard to believe. Two days after the bank robbery I was on the job as a welder for my company that manufactured steel gates, security grills, and fire-escape stairs. My boss called me and said, "Get into the car. We're going to measure a job. We have to make some security grills for a bank." I recognised the route we were taking as the same route to the bank that I had robbed two days before. Sure enough we stopped outside the bank and I balked. "I can't go in there! No way can I go in there!" My boss looked at me and his expression changed. "Don't tell me you robbed this bank the other day!"

I said, "OK, I won't tell you then, but I can't go in there!"

We drove back to work and my boss went back to the bank with someone else. I knew my boss was now aware of my involvement with the organisation but he was afraid to say anything to me about it. He knew it could cost him his life.

A few months later I robbed a post office. My friend and I walked in with guns and ordered everyone to lie on the floor. While my friend held a gun on them, I jumped over the counter and emptied the money from the tills. Within two minutes we were out of the post office and escaped in a stolen car. I casually went to get a haircut and on to work. Robberies were becoming a regular part of my life now.

Another unusual event happened the afternoon of the post office robbery. I went to the home of my boss so I had an alibi in case I needed one. His friend, a post office worker, came through the front door shouting about getting robbed that morning. He said he was frightened because he had £300 in his hand when the robbers entered the post office. When he was told to lie on the floor, (by me!) he lay on top of the money. He smiled at me and said, "I'd love to see that gunman's face if he knew he missed that money." I tried to smile back at him and thought to myself, *mister if you only knew the truth, you wouldn't be laughing now!* Little did he know it was that gunman he was telling his story to!

In the back of my mind the thought was always there that I would eventually be caught by the police and returned to prison. However I would not let my mind dwell on that possibility. I never talked to my wife about what lay ahead, I didn't care – I didn't want to stop. I believed in what I was doing. It was for the Protestant Cause!

My worst fears came true. One night the security forces raided our house moments after I arrived home. I ran out the back door and vaulted into a hedgerow to hide. One of the policemen spotted me and pulled me out and forced me on the

I believed in what I was doing. It was for the Protestant Cause!

ground. He pulled my arms behind my back and handcuffed me. I was defiant and shouted over my shoulder to my wife, "Don't worry! I'll be back soon!" I had a flashback. That's what I had said to her the last time I was arrested! She remembered too. One of the policemen shook his head and said, "Son, it's going to be a long, long time before you're back." I didn't answer him but had a strange feeling that he was telling the truth. He was! This time it would be five years before I would see my old neighbourhood again.

Chapter Eight

BACK IN PRISON

I was taken to the Police Interrogation Centre which is based in Ladus Drive in East Belfast. I found out all of our members apart from one were all in this place. Over the next lot of days, we were interrogated and questioned about everything you can imagine. Murders, bombings, all kinds of armed robberies. I was amazed at the information they had. They actually quoted sentences I had said to others at certain times. It didn't take long to figure out someone had turned informer. It didn't take long either to work out who it was. One of our members had been arrested for something else and they were able to persuade him it would be in his best interest to work for them. He was never charged for anything: they gave him a large amount of money and he moved away to live in another country.

Eventually we were all charged with various crimes, in fact we were inter-charged with each other. They were serious charges and if found guilty we all knew we were facing a long time in prison. We were moved to Crumlin Road jail and put on remand to await our trial. When we finally got together, we discussed every detail. It was beyond doubt who had informed on us. We all tried for bail; I actually prayed and asked God to help me get bail. I had sworn if I got bail I would shoot this guy dead the very same day. I was keen to do it; the truth was we all were keen to kill him. At this time he was still around outside. But at the bail court we all were refused bail; the charges against us were so serious and the police actually blocked any hope we had of any of us being granted bail. We were all remanded back to jail.

My second time in prison was a nightmare especially those first few months. You can't stop thinking about outside. Constantly your thoughts are: *what would I be doing now if I were out?* or – especially at the weekend *Where would I be tonight if I were out?* These are the thoughts of most single men for the first six months after being locked up. Then "inside" becomes your normal lifestyle and you kind of forget about what you did when you were free.

But for the married man it's worse, the thoughts are: *Will my marriage survive?* You just don't know. My thoughts changed to, *I wonder where she is tonight, will she be out to the bar, who's she with?* Such thoughts almost drive you crazy! I saw many married men who were seen as tough guys outside, yet they cracked up because they couldn't cope with the pressures of being inside. Most married men who go into jail have this fear although they may not acknowledge it. I believe it lingers in the back of their minds.

Most of my weekends on the outside were spent drinking with the boys. I never went shopping with my wife and only rarely did I take her out for a drink. I would use the excuse, "if I had more money I'd take you out more," but in reality, I preferred to be out with my friends more than I did with her. A lot of times I would stay away all weekend and come home on Sunday evening. But then, I didn't see it as being wrong really; I knew it wasn't good either but I always made sure my wife got her share of my wages. So to me that made it all right.

I remember having a conversation one day with my wife while I was in remand, I said to her, "At least we had a good relationship outside." I was shocked by her answer. "It was good for you, not for me. You think because you sent money home to feed us that made a good relationship. We had no relationship, you just did your own thing." I was hearing the hard truth now.

"Why didn't you tell me this outside?" I asked. She shook her head and answered, "David I tried to, but YOU never took the time to listen to me."

We were allowed three half-hour visits per week while I waited for sentencing. The visits were the highlight of my week. I missed most the privacy I had enjoyed with my wife. Privacy is a foreign word in prison. It was hard to talk with my wife about any serious subject because another prisoner and his visitors were just a metre away listening to everything said. There were times I watched my wife leave in tears, because of the lack of privacy and the tension we felt knowing others heard everything we said. Every prisoner knew the feeling. Most of the time the conversation is only small talk; you can't say what is really on your mind and you can't express how you really feel. This applies to the wives as well as the husbands. Many times I've seen a prisoner return to his cell with his head hung low and not speak to anyone. The usual comment, if any, would be, "He's had a bad visit."

There were times I watched my wife leave in tears, because of the lack of privacy.

It seemed impossible for any marriage to survive with one partner in prison for a long time. I can count on my hands the small number of marriages that did last. After my sentencing, visits were limited to just 30 minutes per week. That's only 26 hours per year to talk to your wife, the equivalent of slightly more than one day. I knew the chances of my marriage surviving were slim. I had not been able to maintain a good relationship on the outside; how could I survive an eleven-year stretch on 30 minutes each week? This is when you know you're doing time.

A full-scale riot broke out because visits were cancelled after the IRA murdered a prison governor.

That's why visitation was always a point of contention between prisoners and the authorities. Once a full-scale riot broke out because visits were cancelled after the IRA murdered a prison governor as he had just left the prison. I had actually spoken to him just before lunch. He had passed through the prison laundry and saw me with a note in my hand, he thought it must be a smuggled note from a prisoner in another part of the jail so he asked to see it. In fact all it was, was a note of my laundry wash, to inform me which item of clothing belonged to whom. It was hard for me to believe that this poor man was murdered just an hour later.

Because of his murder we were kept locked up in our cells (this is the usual procedure in all prisons in Northern Ireland after a staff murder.) The following day was Saturday and lot of guys were expecting a visit. But they were cancelled too. Many of the prisoners' families and friends had travelled quite a distance only to find the visits cancelled. That made a lot of men very unhappy – including me. When we eventually got out of our cells to go down to the canteen for our supper a lot of guys were shouting that we should protest, so we decided not to lock up again until we got to speak to the wing governor to voice our complaint. After almost an hour of shouting, the Governor arrived. He came into the dining hall and told us to lock up or else. He refused to even give us a hearing but insisted we go back to our cells. I was really angry at this point and as he turned to walk out I lifted my chair and threw it at his back. This was all some of the guys needed to react, within seconds the place was being smashed up. I jumped up onto the table and started to smash the lights. Tables were over turned and legs were broken off as weapons. At this point I just didn't care what the consequences were. I just vented my anger and frustration. As always I expressed myself the way I knew best: with violence.

We built barricades with the broken tables and chairs in front of the iron gates to prevent the riot squad from entering the area. Quietness settled down over the entire prison. We knew it was the calm before the storm. Surely the screws were planning to attack us most likely through the large steel door at the top of the dining hall. A screeching sound told us that the bar that held the door was being pulled back. The door swung open. Someone shouted, "Get ready, they're coming in the top door!"

I turned and faced the doorway and looked through gaps in the barricade. I held a steel table leg in one hand and three darts in the other. I was shocked when I realised the faces I saw were not prison officers. It was the army! A soldier put a gun through the bars, took aim, and fired at me. The rubber baton hit me in the shoulder and spun me around. We all tried to find cover behind chairs or tables. I turned and threw the three darts toward the crowd of soldiers and officers who were charging us. Suddenly I was knocked to the floor by a strong jet of cold water. I could hardly breathe! I thought I would drown if the water didn't stop. I gasped for air and felt the heel of a boot on my throat. I choked as I looked past the boot to see a soldier enjoying his conquest of me. He raised the visor on his helmet and gave me an evil smile. He took a rubber bullet out of his belt, loaded his gun, and placed the muzzle within two inches of my face. I heard the click as he cocked the gun.

"Please mister, don't!" I begged. He smiled again and moved the gun down, pointing it between my legs.

I pleaded with him not to shoot me. He moved the gun to my thigh and pulled the trigger. The pain was unbearable. My leg felt like it was on fire, as if someone had stuck a hot poker into me. I thought for sure it was broken. The force of the shot spun me around on the floor. As I cried out in pain an officer came across the room and kicked me and told me to stand against the wall. Some of my friends helped me to my feet and prevented me from falling. I stood on one leg with my nose pressed against the wall. If we looked around, a soldier used a baton across the back of our heads or crushed our fingers on the wall. One by one we were led into the 'bunk', a cell used by prison staff as an office. There we met the prison doctor, famous for standing by the wall with his hands behind him. I never knew anyone who had ever been actually examined by him.

David Hamilton a year before he went to prison.

David and Liam outside David's house in Rathcoole in 1984.

A typical cell in Crumlin Road jail.

One of the wings in Crumlin Road Jail.

David outside the courthouse on Crumlin Road.

David revisits compounds with ex-republican Tom Kelly.

David with his wife Sharon and his sister Joy inside the padded cell in the H-Blocks.

David points to one of the names inscribed on the prison wall.

David back in the dock – 25 years later.

David looking through the cell window again.

David back in his cell again where he was converted in Crumlin Road Jail.

A dream come true – together with Sharon in the cell.

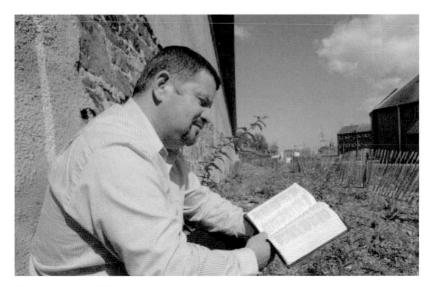

David reads his bible in the prison graveyard.

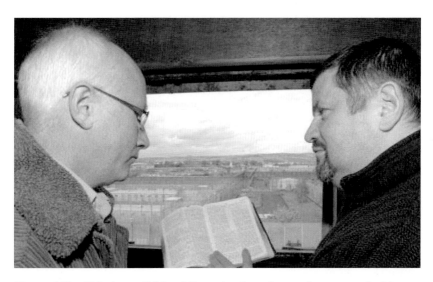

Tom and David look at a Bible while gazing from the watch tower overlooking the H-Blocks.

James and Margaret McIlroy.

Mum and Revd Jackson Buick.

David and Sharon on their wedding day.

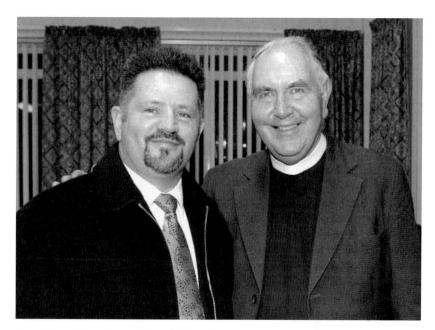

Revd David Jardine with David Hamilton.

The doctor asked me, "What's wrong with you?" I knew from my past experience with the doctor what his standard answer would be, as always, "You need a three-day lock-up." So I knew not to expect any help from the doctor. My thigh was swollen to twice its normal size it was obvious for everyone to see what my problem was. "Let's see this leg, pull your trousers down," the doctor impatiently requested. My thigh was black and blue and there was a perfect circle where the bullet hit me. He asked, "How did you do this?" I told him it wasn't me who did it but a soldier, but he chose not to believe me.

"Now, this is when the fun starts, Hamilton! You have to run the gauntlet."

His conclusion was that the wound was self-inflicted and that I needed to be locked up for a few days. I was expecting this kind of response from him, so I just said, "Thanks, doc, it's nice to know someone cares!" I held onto the wall and hobbled out of the cell.

A screw said, "Now, this is when the fun starts, Hamilton! You have to run the gauntlet." I looked down the wing and saw what he meant. Prison officers were lined up double all the way to the bottom of the stairs. They would issue their own punishment to us! I just smiled at him. I can honestly say I wasn't the least bit afraid – violence and pain were a big part of my life; I just accepted it. Outside, whenever the police would have you in a cell, most times they would give you a beating. When they did beat me, the more determined I was not to break. So most times the beatings actually caused me to hate authority even more.

I made no attempt to run, I could barely walk; I started to pass through the middle of them. Some of them were screaming in delight as they began to beat me with their batons. I tried to protect my face as best I could. I felt blood running down my neck after a strong blow to the head. Eventually I reached the bottom of the stairs, my beating stopped at the same time I heard someone behind me scream as the screws began to batter him. I struggled to the top of the landing and limped to my cell. I wiped the blood off with my towel and changed into dry clothes. I collapsed on my bed and looked across at my cellmate. He had a wet face cloth over his face. "How many bumps have you?" he asked, with a laugh. He stopped laughing when he saw the mess my leg was in. He couldn't believe it!

Today, seventeen years later, I still carry the indent in my thigh where that soldier shot me with that rubber bullet. I would never have believed it back then but I was to meet this very soldier again. He would later read the first edition of this book and come to Manchester to visit me! It took quite a while for things to settle down. Some prisoners collected names of the screws who did most of the beatings and these were sent out to paramilitaries to be dealt with. One of the worst officers involved was a Welshman; he *enjoyed* beating you with a truncheon. He would scream in delight as he battered you. If anyone was a sadist he fitted the description. I cannot say it was a surprise to me to learn he was shot a few weeks later. Fortunately for him, he survived it.

I was glad when my trial was finally set. I spent a lot of time talking to my barrister about the trial. He told me I would probably be sentenced to at least five years more than the others who had been involved with me in the bank and post office robberies. He thought the others might get up to ten years and that I would get hit even harder.

When I walked into the courtroom I wasn't terribly pleased to find out the judge was the same judge who sentenced me a few years before. That was all I needed! My brain was overwhelmed by the memory of the judge telling me he never wanted to see me again. The judge first sentenced my friend. He got 12 years! My mind was racing, if he got 12 years, how many would I get? I was calculating in my head if what my barrister said was right, I would be serving an 16-18 year stretch! When the judge called out my name, I apprehensively stood up, expecting the worst. It seemed like an eternity as all my charges were read out. I had already pleaded guilty; now I would know the sentence. I got five years for this, then eight years for that; ten years for something else, I wasn't so much interested in the charges, it was the sentences I was listening to. Whatever the largest sentence was, that would be the one that I would have to serve. What about my five-year licence? As I feared, the judge referred to it before he announced his final decision. Some of our relatives were crying in the public gallery by this stage.

"Hamilton," the judge started slowly, "it's obvious you relied a lot on team work to accomplish these crimes. Therefore I feel it would be wrong of me to sentence you to more than the others. I sentence you to 12 years also!" Because of the severity of the sentencing, one of my comrades decided to change his plea to "not guilty;" because of this our sentence was reduced to eleven years. Unfortunately for him, at his retrial his previous sentence was greatly increased!

We were brought back to the waiting cells beneath the courts, a screw removed our handcuffs. We were all in a state of shock. It took a minute before someone broke the silence. My mate banged the wall with his fist. "That judge was bad news!" he exclaimed. Fifteen minutes later my mother was allowed in to see me. She was crying and very upset. She said "David, what is going to happen to you? You don't care; you're throwing your life away!" I was trying to argue with her. "It's for the Cause," I answered, but she wasn't having it.

My mate banged the wall with his fist. "That judge was bad news!"

"You don't care about anyone, me, your wife or son? Do you?" she went on to say. "All you think about is the UVF – you're a hopeless case! You will never change!"

I was embarrassed by all this; it was happening in front of others. "Mum, just go home, please." I turned away from her, indicating I didn't want to speak to her any further. After a moment she turned toward the door and the screw opened it for her to go out. I give her a quick glance as she went. I could still hear her sobbing before the cell door closed. Our barrister eventually came down to the cell with a sheepish look on his face. He couldn't explain the long sentences. He said the judge showed no leniency at all, except to me. He turned to me and said, "You got off light – you should be happy." I answered, "You don't see me laughing, do you?" He looked me straight in the eyes and said, "You should be: someone must have been praying for you." I grumbled, "I don't think so." Years later I would find out that someone had been praying for me. A precious old woman whose prayers would change my life.

Chapter Nine

IN THE H-BLOCKS

The moment we were sentenced we were told, "You will no longer be treated as political prisoners." Now we were seen as criminals. Special Category Status by this time had been removed by the British government to paramilitary prisoners in Northern Ireland's prisons. The policy was phased out for existing sentenced political prisoners; they remained the same, until their sentence was served. They were housed in the old part of the prison, known as Long Kesh. And the new part was HMP Maze. It was here the new policy was introduced for those newly convicted.

After the trial was over we all were moved to the Maze prison. Now we had to wear prison uniforms. The Maze was commonly known as the H-blocks. All newly sentenced prisoners were housed in H-block 7. I did not know what to expect, it had a bad reputation for being very strict. The screws let us know who was in charge of the place. The block was kept immaculately clean; the tile floor was constantly washed, polished and buffed. The toilets were kept spotless, even the toilet seats were polished. The black plastic bins were also given the same treatment so that they were gleaming too. This was the discipline block, specifically set up to teach prisoners strict discipline. We were constantly reminded that we were now sentenced prisoners – criminals. No longer political prisoners, no more special privileges, you did whatever the screws told you to do.

The blocks were all built in the shape of the letter "H" with four wings. The centre bar was for the administration office. I didn't like living in "The Blocks" at all. The exercise yard was depressing. It was a square yard enclosed on every side by corrugated fencing four metres high, you could see nothing, only four tin walls. A highlight for us was to see an aeroplane flying high across the sky; it helped to break the monotony. Exercise was like walking around the inside of a huge biscuit tin.

After a month in the discipline block I was moved across to H-6 where I expected things to be a little easier. I was aware Republicans and Loyalists were all living together now. It was here I saw my first Blanket man. These were IRA and INLA prisoners who began what was known as the Blanket protest in which prisoners would refuse to wear prison uniform or to wash and shave, they ripped a hole in their prison blanket and wore it as a poncho. On many occasions I witnessed these men being treated so badly by the screws that I felt pity for them. But still they refused to give in, regardless how many beatings they got. This then escalated into the dirty protest where these same prisoners not only refused to wash they began to smear the walls of their cells with excrement. Because we were all together side by side down the wing, I can remember the stench that came from these dirty cells, many times I watched the maggots crawl out from under the cell door. Even the maggots wanted out of there. These protests were aimed to

Many times I watched the maggots crawl out from under the cell door.

re-establish their political privileges by securing what were known as the 'Five Demands': The Right not to wear a prison uniform; The Right not to do prison work; The Right of free association with other prisoners; The Right to organise their own educational and recreational facilities; The Right to one visit, one letter and one parcel per week.

A number of Loyalist prisoners also started their own protest, but after a few weeks, the Loyalist leaders thought it would be a lot easier just to wait and see what the outcome would be, perhaps we could win concessions on the backs of Republicans. It was hard to watch.

I saw them many a time being dragged from their cells by their hair, and their cells hosed down and them too. All the glass in their cell windows were smashed out by the screws using their batons so they had to endure the elements too. Later on they had a steel perforated plate put over these cell windows. The harsh treatment these men had to endure was unbelievable.

Despite all of this happening the prison authorities were trying to keep some sign of normality going. I got allocated a job in the prison laundry and I was happy about this. It was a good number because it had plenty of perks. It meant I was able to wear the best of prison garb including a denim waistcoat over my blue and white pinstripe shirt and grey denim trousers. As a laundry worker I had a little more freedom than the normal prisoner as I had to pick up and deliver laundry. I enjoyed my visits to the prison kitchen because I usually came back with more than dirty clothes. One day I filled the laundry bag with all kinds of goodies.

As I walked toward the door to return to the laundry the PO (principal officer) stopped me. "Let me see inside your bag," he ordered. I didn't know what to do. I knew I was in big trouble and would probably be sent to "the boards" – the slang expression for the punishment block. I fumbled with the string on the bag until food started falling out. A whole assortment of cooked meat fell out onto the floor. This was followed by six hard-boiled eggs, two tomatoes, an onion, a half-loaf of bread and a huge chunk of corned beef!

The PO went berserk! He started shouting, "Get out of my kitchen! Don't ever come back in here! Do you hear me?"

"Yes sir!" I yelled and rushed off toward the gate. The screw opened the grill as he saw me coming, "Hamilton, you're lucky he let you off."

After that experience they always sent another prisoner to collect the kitchen laundry. It wasn't only with the prison staff that I had problems, either; one other time it was with the leaders of my own paramilitary group. Like the time I took a notion to carve an Irish harp. I really enjoyed handicrafts. I worked as an orderly at that time. One day I was sent out to clean a classroom. The blackboard on the wall was enclosed by a mahogany wood surround and I thought, "That wood would make a nice harp!" I spent an hour cutting all the wood of the mahogany frame from of the blackboard and smuggled it into my cell. I learned the next day that both the prison authorities and the prisoner's council were upset and had begun an investigation. The trail led directly to my cell!

Those screws in charge of the block left it up to my fellow

prisoners to deal with me. I was told by my own to remain locked in my cell until a court-martial trial could be set up. I was charged with destroying prisoner's property, a severe offence. That afternoon I was taken to the classroom and met by four prisoners sitting at a table. The four were in charge of each of the wings of our block. I was worried because one of these men was the Commanding Officer of all the Loyalists in the Maze. It was well known he had been responsible for the murders of several people outside prison. It was also rumoured that he poisoned his cell mate the year before. I didn't think I would be killed for stealing the wood from around the blackboard, but I was still nervous as to what my punishment might be. I sat down and one of the men said, "As you can see Davey, there's no blackboard in here. What happened to it?" I told them the truth. They asked me to wait outside while they decided my punishment. When they called me back inside, the main man said, "We've decided to give you the benefit of the doubt. You're new here and we're letting you off light. Your punishment is to be locked up for a week, no recreation, no yard time." I was thankful that my first brush with prison justice ended OK.

I was charged with destroying prisoner's property, a severe offence.

Being locked up was no problem. I spent the time in my cell working on my harp. No one had mentioned the wood, so I kept it.

About the time I was beginning to get used to being in H-6. I was suddenly transferred to Belfast Prison, the 'Crum'. I was placed in 'D' wing, the part of the prison reserved for prisoners serving long sentences. It was not a happy place!

Some of the most hardened criminals were in 'D' wing, including sex offenders who would have been beaten or killed in the Blocks. I was not a happy person being moved here on my own. I think it was because I had got into trouble in the Blocks I was being punished and sent back to the Crum.

Suddenly one afternoon I was out of there. I felt all eyes on me at supper that night. Again I was the new kid on the block. I felt better when a guy shouted, "Davey, bring your grub over here and sit down." It was a prisoner named Edge, one of the leading Loyalists in the prison. We had been in the compounds together a few years before. It was important to be recognised. At least it gave me some status. It was easier for my wife and family to visit me in Belfast Prison since the prison was only 20 minutes from my home. I landed a job in the laundry again. I had learned the prison work ethic: do as little as you can, as often as you can. The prison laundry was old. The machines dated from the beginning of the century, (which century was debatable). We delivered laundry around the prison in huge blue baskets. It was a great way to smuggle contraband.

Prisoners who wanted a special touch for their clothing paid us off in food, or tobacco, the most used method of payment in prison, pornographic literature was not allowed but it could be got occasionally. The handicrafts were better in Belfast prison than the Maze: there was much more room. We had a good size workshop purely for this purpose, whereas down below we had to do crafts in a regular cell. This meant only two or three could work in it, so the custom was to make the things in your own cell. This wasn't good especially if you were sanding wood or sawing it up: your cell would be full of sawdust. Whoever designed the H-blocks had one thing in his mind: to make a cell for men to stay in. He wasn't told these men will be let out to have recreation, so he didn't plan anywhere for men to work at their hobbies. I began to do the leather work up there; it was something I got a lot of pleasure from. I paid another inmate to teach me the basics and began by making small items, such as lighter cases with guys initials on them or made a belt to learn the stamping techniques. Then I expanded to larger items like purses with beautiful carved designs. These became really popular. Some of the leather work that came out of the prisons in Northern Ireland are real works of art, the carving techniques acknowledged by leather workers around the world.

Over the years I've made everything from Bible covers to gun holsters. It was common for officers to ask someone to make handbags or other things for their wives. There were only a few masterworkers who each had their own secrets but over the years they taught me. It was a great way to pass the time away.

Chapter Ten

INTO THE LIGHT

"Any volunteers to read a prayer?" the prison chaplain, Rev Robert Russell, asked during the Thursday afternoon chapel service. We went to church just to have something to do! No one volunteered to pray. Someone shouted, "The last time I volunteered for anything I got ten years in prison!" Everyone laughed. The chaplain looked straight at me and asked, "How about you Davey?" I would try anything once so I told him OK. He handed me a small piece of paper with a prayer poem written on it. When I stood up to read it one of my mates grabbed the back of my leg to make me scream. Somehow I managed not to!

When I finished reading the prayer I felt good inside. I couldn't explain it. I wrote to my mother that night and told her how good it was to say a prayer in church. Only God could have known that in less than a year I would be doing much more than praying in church! I heard that my friend Big Billy had become a Christian. He was a bit crazy anyway, only now he was completely crazy. No one I knew in jail was interested in God. We went to church to hear "all the scale" (new news) not because any one had time for God. I couldn't see big Billy staying a Christian for long. I just laughed.

I remember it was New Year's Eve and I was sharing a cell with a crazy guy with the nickname Crazy Horse. That night a few minutes before midnight we took our steel feet off our beds to bang the steel door with. In jail, this was our way of seeing the new year in. At the stroke of midnight as car horns are sounded all across the city the ships in the harbour are blowing their huge horns. It is a time of festivity, so even in jail we celebrate it. Usually what happens is that all the men shout out from the side of the doors and make as much noise as possible. I can remember standing at the door banging it as hard as I could. I thought to myself: *This new year will be no different from last year or the year before.* Things never change in any big way in the prison, even the food is the same each week. Yet before the first month of the new year would be over, my life would be changed completely.

It was the 28th January 1980. As always, I got myself a cup of hot water to bring into my cell, to make a cup of tea. We were banging up for the night. When I pulled my cell door shut, I saw a small piece of paper lying on my bed. I asked my cell mate what it was. He told me it was a Christian tract. I just laughed, picked it up, looked at the front page, and read it out loud, "Jesus Christ is coming back soon." I turned and said to my cell-mate, "To a cinema near you!" We both laughed. Like most guys in jail, I wasn't interested in anything to do with religion. So I screwed the tract up into a ball, and threw it out of the window. I sat down on my bed to drink my tea and never gave the tract any more thought.

While I was sitting there something strange happened. I had this thought come into my mind, *it's time for you to change, to become a Christian.* I was startled by this; it was so strange. Never in my life had I ever thought to be a Christian. I took another drink of my tea. A few moments later, I had the same thought again – *Become a Christian.* This time I laughed out loud and my cell mate asked, "What are you laughing about?"

"Nothing." I answered. I knew he wouldn't believe me if I told him, so I said nothing. Even if I wanted to be a real Christian I thought for sure God would not be interested in someone like me. I thought I was too far gone to ever change. I knew I was bad, and I'd been involved in some bad things. The organisation I belonged to had killed many people. Some of my best friends were murderers. It wasn't because they were any worse than me; it was just the way things happened to turn out. I had not taken anyone's life, but it wasn't for the want of trying. I knew it was a miracle that I was not serving a life sentence too. I could recall times when I left my house with murder on my mind. Now I can say I am truly thankful to God it never took place. But I knew I was a violent man at times and also a robber and a thief. Surely God had no time for people like me!

I shook myself back to reality and put my cup upon the bookshelf, beside a Bible. (There is a Bible in every cell, thanks to a Christian organisation called "Gideons International," who distribute Bibles into schools, hotels and prisons in most of the countries of the world). In fact, all the guys in jail like the Bible; if you run out of cigarette papers it's the next best thing – you just rip a page out of it! I guess I'd smoked Matthew, Mark, Luke and John over the years!

I looked at the Bible as if seeing it for the first time; I lifted it down and began to flick the pages, reading a few lines here and there. It didn't make any sense at all so I put it back on the shelf. A few minutes later, I pulled it back down again, opened it and tried to read for the second time. It still didn't make much sense so I put it back again. I really felt uncomfortable, as if something was bothering me. I was starting to feel agitated for no reason.

I sat back on my bed looking at this Bible, then I thought to myself, *Didn't I hear the Minister say you should always pray before reading the Bible?* So I lifted the Bible down, sat back on the bed with the Bible sitting on my knees and I actually prayed a silent prayer asking God to help me read the Bible. That was all I prayed. I opened it for the third time and began to read and after a few lines it still didn't seem to make any sense. "What are you doing with that Bible?" Crazy Horse asked. I didn't know what to answer. Sheepishly I said, "I am thinking about being a Christian." Of course he began to laugh, "You a Christian! No way." He lay back on his bed laughing, "You need a good night's sleep, you will be normal again tomorrow!"

"You need a good night's sleep, you will be normal again tomorrow!"

I was in the middle of a snooker competition and I had actually reached the finals, it was between a guy called Jojo and me to see who would win the prize of tobacco. Funny, before lock-up it was the only thing on my mind, now it didn't seem to be of any importance if I won or not. I thought, *my mate is right, this is crazy, tomorrow I will have forgotten all about this.* So I rolled a cigarette and lay back on the bed.

Anyway God would have no time for the likes of me, he's only interested in good people, the sort who go to church and listen to 'Batman'. (As a child, when I first went to church and saw the minister all dressed up in black, with a robe. I thought it was Batman. Two years later I found out it wasn't – man, I was disappointed!)

While lying on my bed I started to think about my life, the way I lived outside. Now it seemed crazy. Maybe there is a better way to live, but where do you find it? As a Christian? I doubted that, it had no appeal to me at all. Prison was bad, but church was worse! No life in being a Christian: I reasoned that it must be terribly boring to be a Christian – no more smoking, drinking, or partying.

My next thought was those things never truly satisfy anyway. Then I began to have these strange thoughts about times in my life when I could have died. I thought about the night when I was out with my fiancée having a meal and the IRA attempted to kill me – for sure that was a near miss. I was lucky, or so I thought, maybe it was more than luck. What about the time my bomb exploded prematurely while I was still in the building! I thought about that night. I woke lying on the ground with broken glass all around me. Although my jacket was cut to shreds I couldn't find so much as a scratch on my body. How did I survive that? It must have been God! What about the time I was shot while up the Shankill? Three bullets in me! Not many live to tell such tales, so why was I still alive? The thought rushed through my brain, *It was God who kept me alive all those times!* There was really no other explanation, but why? If God wasn't interested in people like me, then surely he would have let me die. So what was the reason for sparing my life? What could it be? Could God change my life after all?

I was feeling confused now, and these thoughts continued

until I finally fell asleep. The next morning when I awoke, my first thought was: *Become a Christian!* The thoughts were still there! I knew I had to make some kind of a decision soon because this Christian thing was beginning to bother me now. I still felt it was time for me to change but I didn't know exactly how to do that. But I was soon to discover that God always puts people in our pathway to help us find His will for our lives. The right person for me was close by! I worked in the prison laundry with a man nicknamed the 'Wee Man'. 'Wee Man' (Trevor was his proper name) had been a Christian for eight years and was famous for sticking gospel tracts inside trouser and shirt pockets in the laundry. I admired him because he had the guts to distribute the tracts, but I still thought he was crazy. Many times I had seen him put gospel tracts inside the clothes. This would make men mad. Many times they would threaten him to try to make him stop, but the 'Wee Man' just kept on. He always carried gospel tracts in his pockets. In the laundry it would be really hot and steamy, everyone was always perspiring. One day I saw a screw take his hat off and sat it down on the table to wipe his brow with a handkerchief. I saw 'Wee Man' move close to the table. Next thing he stuck something inside the brim of the screw's hat and walked away. A minute later when the screw placed his hat back on his head he immediately took it off again to see what was inside. From out of the brim he pulled out a gospel tract! I thought it was so funny!

As I was going down to go to work that morning someone was blocking the stairs. It was the 'Wee Man!' He turned and spoke to me. The next words out of my mouth surprised even me, "Wee Man, I'm thinking about becoming a Christian, but I don't know what to do." I thought he would laugh at me because I had mocked him so many times for being a Christian. Instead he walked up to me and put his arms around me and hugged me. I was embarrassed! I was glad none of the other prisoners were around! That kind of action is easily misinterpreted in prison. The 'Wee Man' gave me several tracts – enough reading material for a month!

During a break in the laundry I asked the 'Wee Man' questions about being a Christian. Someone shouted, "Look at Davey talking to the Sky Pilot." 'Sky Pilot' was one of our mocking names for Christians. I was embarrassed and asked the 'Wee Man' to meet me in the toilet to talk. The 'Wee Man' prayed with me and asked God to show me how to get saved, and before he left, he gave me more tracts! I went back to my cell during lunch and I made up my mind that it was time to turn my life over to Christ. I read one of the 'Wee Man's' tracts that had a simple prayer:

That's it! I thought. I'm now a Christian!

Come into my heart Lord Jesus, come into my heart today.
Come into my heart Lord Jesus, come into my heart to stay.

I prayed the prayer six times just to make sure God knew I was serious! *That's it!* I thought. *I'm now a Christian!* My cell mate woke up and asked me what I was smiling about. I said, "I've just become a Christian!" He snarled at me and used a few curse words to tell me how he felt about my decision. When the cell door opened for us to return to work he started yelling, "Davey's a Christian now! He's joined the God Squad!" Another prisoner shouted, "Hallelujah!"

The first person I saw was Jojo who I was supposed to play in a snooker game that night. I told him, "Jojo, I can't play snooker tonight because it's for tobacco, it's gambling and Christians don't gamble!" He laughed and walked on without answering. It ended up I did play and actually won that night. I got a bounty bar as a prize. That must have been my first miracle – I don't think I ever won another game after that!

As I continued walking down the landing someone else yelled out, "Tonight Davey will perform his first miracle, he's going to walk on the bath water!" a lot of guys were laughing now. So did I! That afternoon on the way over to work, I spotted the Chaplain Rev Bill Vance. I shouted over to him, "I am a Christian now!" He stopped and walked back to me. "When did this happen?" he asked. He then told me to follow him back to the wing. In the office he asked me to tell him what happened, so I told him as best I could. He just sat and smiled, when I'd finished he got up and opened a cupboard and gave me my first Bible, a little red New Testament. He prayed for me before I went back to the laundry. I felt ten feet tall! It was the first time I heard anyone personally praying for me.

"Tonight Davey will perform his first miracle, he's going to walk on the bath water!"

What I didn't know then was that God had someone else praying for David Hamilton's salvation. He had placed me on the heart of an 83-year-old lady named Annie Beggs, my uncle's mother-in-law. I never knew Mrs. Beggs personally before my conversion. As a boy occasionally I would hear my mum mention her in conversation, but she knew me OK!

On the day I was sentenced to prison she spoke to my mother who was sitting crying about her hopeless son. Mum said I was a hopeless case, that all I lived for was the UVF, and that I would never change. Mrs. Beggs shook her head and told Mum, "God can change your son." Mum disagreed and shook her head in despair. Mrs. Beggs continued, "If God could change the heart of John Newton (who after his conversion composed the hymn "Amazing Grace") he can change the heart of your son. I will put him on my prayer list and pray for him every day, I promise you," she said.

At that time she was in her eighties! An amazing woman for her age, she had all her faculties about her and spent most of her nights in prayer. When she said she was praying about something she meant it. She was known by many as a woman of prayer. A well-known Professor in a Belfast hospital would come to seek her advice on many things, because once he himself had to go into hospital for heart surgery. He was unsure because the medical people had told him there was only a 50% chance of it working. It could actually go either way. Annie told him she would pray about it first and then let him know what she thought he should do. She later told him she had prayed and God had given her assurance it would be successful and she felt he should go ahead with the operation, which he did. It was a great success and amazed the surgeon and staff involved in the operation, as they watched the speed of his recovery. The Professor said it was because Annie Beggs had been praying for him!

Two years later God miraculously answered the prayers of Annie Beggs this time on my behalf. When I got converted, it was the talk of the whole wing. I knew that I would be the butt of all the jokes when I showed up in the dining hall that evening. Sure enough Jojo stood up on a chair and announced, "Since Davey is a Christian now he can pray for our food!" Everyone laughed, except me. I was a nice shade of purple! Above the laughter he said, "Everyone bow your heads, all eyes closed. Davey, pray!" I set my tray down on the table in front of me, bowed my head and said a short prayer. When I opened my eyes I discovered my sausages were gone from off my tray! It didn't stop me praying though; I continued to pray for all my meals after that, but I always made sure I kept one eye open!

That night I wrote to my parents to tell them about my conversion. I later found out that my mother had cried as she read my letter out, and my father was almost crying too. He said, "Poor son, he's gone mad in prison." My mother was so moved that she decided to accept Christ two days later. She could hardly wait to visit Granny Beggs (as my mum called her) to tell her the good news. Before Mum could tell Granny anything, Granny said, "I know why you're here! David has become a Christian!" She told Mum that God had lifted the burden for my salvation from her heart the night I got saved. Now, she said, God has told me to pray for his future ministry!

"Everyone bow your heads, all eyes closed. Davey, pray!"

I went to my first prison prayer meeting a few days after I got saved. I was embarrassed because there were several prisoners there who I had ridiculed in a terrible way for their stand as Christians, just three nights before. I knew they did not take me seriously; they found it hard to accept that I was truly converted. There were several sex-offenders present in the meeting. I couldn't accept them either as being Christians and they knew it! About the only person glad to see me was the Chaplain, the Rev David Jardine who announced, "It's nice to see you David. Take a seat. We're reading from Galatians." I often tried to be witty so I asked, "Is that some place in Belfast?" I was the only person laughing. One of the men turned to his friend and said, "I knew he wasn't saved!" I felt stupid for not being more serious. I made another blunder about 15 minutes later. I was so relaxed in the Bible study that I took a cigarette tin out of my pocket and began to roll a smoke. All eyes were on me! I thought, *this is not right. A Christian shares things with others and I haven't even offered anyone else a cigarette!* So I stood up and offered my tin around. I was surprised when no one accepted.

The chaplain kindly said, "David you can't smoke in here. This is a Bible study." "Oh," I said and put the roll-up (cigarette) behind my ear for later. I heard somebody make another comment, "Told you he wasn't saved."

I just smiled. I knew I had a lot to learn now as a Christian.

Chapter Eleven

A PRISON CHRISTIAN

Life in prison is tough at the best of times, but as a Christian it was even tougher! I began to make some new Christian friends while a few fellow prisoners despised me for no longer being a Loyalist. I had made a decision immediately to stop being a member of the UVF. Regardless of the consequences, I felt it was the only thing to do; the truth was, I had to leave now or I could not call myself a Christian.

I cancelled my financial support from them on the outside. I stopped having visits from anyone who was involved with the organisation outside. I told them I was finished with it all, no more taking orders; I would talk to everybody from now on. I soon found out, although God had changed me, that He hadn't changed everyone else. There was a Catholic guy I had had a fight with one time over in the laundry. Since then we stayed out of each other's way. But the same day I made my commitment to Christ I went to him and told him. His answer was, "Why are you telling me this?" I told him, "From now on I will be speaking to everyone. I don't care who they are, or what their crime was."

Another prisoner who was already a Christian, Big D, challenged me to stop smoking. He said it would prove to others that I was serious about serving God. I accepted the challenge. Thank God, I've never had a cigarette since. I know it was a miracle for me to stop smoking. I had tried several times before, but never succeeded. I knew this time it wasn't my own strength I was depending on. I had no craving, like other times before. I didn't even feel tempted for a cigarette.

I was in a guy's cell three days later, when he offered me a cigarette. I refused it and said, "As a Christian now, I don't smoke." He laughed at me and said,

"Davey don't go overboard. As a Christian you can still smoke you know." My reply was: "The Apostle Peter went overboard and he walked on water! So I want to go all the way too!" He had a good laugh over this.

Big D was a genuine Christian. We became good friends and, later on, cell mates. He taught me a lot about studying the Bible and applying the principles I learned to my everyday life, even locked up in a prison. Big D was completely opposite from me. I never cared about how my cell looked but Big D kept the cell immaculate. He even folded his socks before putting them in the cupboard. His side of the bookshelf was clean, mine was full of papers, odds and ends.

I found out that many prisoners were betting on how long I would last as a Christian.

I was in the exercise yard a few days later when one of my friends came over to me and announced, "Davey, I think you're a genuine Christian. Keep it up, I'm betting a half-ounce on you!" I found out that many prisoners were betting on how long I would last as a Christian. It scared me a little, and I confided in my friend Jamie that I didn't think I would make it as a Christian. Although I wanted to I just couldn't see myself lasting as one; I was not strong enough.

I was shocked by his answer, "You're right Davey, you don't have the strength. But God does!" He turned to John 1:12 in his Bible which reads, "To as many as believe in Him God gives them the power to become a son of God." That's what I needed to hear!

The devil doesn't like to let anyone go that easily, as I soon found out. One of the screws came into my cell once and asked me if I was still a Christian. When I replied "Yeah" with a smile, he punched me in the face. I was determined not to react. "Are you still a Christian?" he asked. He punched me again, laughed in my face, and turned and walked out the door. That officer hated me from that day on. He never accepted that my conversion was real. Even when I was eventually released from prison, he told me on my way out that he would keep my cell ready because he knew I would be back! I told him I hoped he was right because I wanted to come back but this time to preach the Gospel to the men who remained locked up!

Neither did it stop there either, the devil had another go at me a week later: this time from a screw that lived in the same area as I did outside. He thought because I was a Christian now, the UVF would have nothing to do with me, or perhaps they would put me on a hit list because I no longer was a member. Whatever the reason, he decided he would give me a hard time. As I came back from work that Monday lunch time, he called me over and told me to strip off. He said he wanted to search me in case I had a weapon or drugs. I knew this wasn't really the case. As I removed my outer clothing he told me to strip naked. He then made me stand there for about fifteen minutes while the other guys went past to their cells. That afternoon coming back onto the landing he called me and did the same thing again. Inside I felt the frustration OK, but I had no anger. Yet looking back I am amazed it never once entered my mind to hit him – had it done so, I would have immediately. I knew the whole wing was watching and waiting to see if I would react with violence. I decided I would just take it and ask God to help me. Of course my mates who were watching all of this said, "Davey, you're crazy; why not send his name outside and the boys will kill him for you?"

I said, "No, I believe God will deal with him about this." He continued to search me each day for the rest of that week. I was waiting for it to start again when I went to work the following Monday morning. I was surprised when I came back onto the landing that dinner hour. He greeted me as a long-lost friend – he was so nice to me I couldn't figure out why. I knew God had answered my prayers, but what I didn't know then was, it was 'with a little help from my friends.' Unknown to me, one of my UVF mates decided to send this man's name out and asked someone to have a talk with him, but not to kill him or I would know. It happened that weekend. This screw was out drinking with another screw in one of the local bars in our area when a few men walked into the toilet behind him and stuck a gun barrel up his nostril and asked him if he knew a friend of theirs called Davey Hamilton. They told him someone had said he was giving me a hard time – of course he denied it. They told him if it didn't stop he would be a dead man because they knew where he lived and could get him any time they wanted. I never had any problems with him after

I decided I would just take it and ask God to help me.

that, but I wasn't to find all this out a year later. Actually it was the screw who had been with him drinking that night that told me the rest of the story.

One of my mates called Big J answered, "Yeah, God works in mysterious ways that's for sure." I was surprised by this, because I knew he claimed he didn't believe in God so I wondered what he meant by it. When I asked him to explain, he just smiled as he got up to leave. He repeated it, "God works in mysterious ways." That was all he said. It was only when I heard the full story later, that I thought back to the conversation in the dining hall and wondered if Big J knew more about it back then than I did.

Not all of the screws made it tough on me. Most of them were easy to get along with and a few became real friends. Some were Christians and helped me grow in the Lord. They slipped tracts under my door and talked to me about the Bible after they finished their rounds. I thank God for the positive influence of those officers who often came along at the right moment when I needed encouragement to continue my Christian walk. Those early days trying to be a Christian in prison were hard for me in many ways. At times I thought, *I'll never make it, I am not one of those particular kinds of people who are meant to be Christian.*

As I began to read my Bible, I found it hard to put it down. Every day I started to spend hours in it. I learned about fasting and decided to miss my lunch. Even though I worked in the laundry (we got food perks!) it wasn't as bad as I thought it would be. I believe God told me to make this part of my life on a regular basis. As I began to do this I could understand why the early Christians practised this discipline and saw things happen. So did I! I began to take it seriously; fasting for a whole day for the first time to me was a great experience, I found it helped me to read the Bible and to get more from it. So I made it part of my routine to fast one day a week. I chose Sunday as this was when we got our best dinner of the whole week, we got chicken or else a slice of steak – I wanted to give my best to God and this was to me my ultimate sacrifice. I maintained this for nearly three months, then I decided to fast for two days after reading that the Pharisees did this, so I changed to Tuesday and Thursday, and again this I kept up for another three months. I found this to be powerful for my prayer life. Over the years I was able to increase this more and more until I could do prolonged fasts of two or three weeks, on those special occasions when I knew I needed to hear from God. As I did this I saw many results of prayer.

Although I was growing as a Christian, it wasn't all plain sailing for me and I started to have trouble with this particular guy who worked along with me. He was always making a mockery of me in front of others and putting me down as an idiot for being a Christian. I usually would just ignore him and laugh it off, but after a while it began to bother me. One particular day he was showing off how strong he was, for sure he was a big guy who worked out a lot in the gym. When he saw me he said to the others that he could let me hit him a punch on the face and he wouldn't even feel it.

That was the wrong thing to say in front of me. Before I had become a Christian, I loved to fight, enjoying the buzz I got this way. I knew how to punch and I knew I could knock him out with one good punch if it connected on the side of his jaw.

Sad to say, I allowed the old man in me to surface and decided I wanted to fight him, much to his surprise. I walked over and said to him, "Let's go out the back, just you and me and everyone can wait to see who comes back in first." Unknown to him I had gone out two minutes before and put a rolling pin at the back door so I was making sure I would win. I had made up my mind; my plan was to break his two arms. It was as if something snapped in my mind and that was all I wanted to do. I hadn't had even one row since my conversion and I had been a Christian now for probably three months. But now it was the 'old man.' I shouted at this guy who was doing all this boasting and called him every name I could think of to try to get him mad. He got afraid, having never seen me like this before, and he began to apologise and said he didn't want to fight. Eventually I walked away. It wasn't long after when I began to feel depressed about my earlier behaviour. So much for being a Christian! I blew it big time. I was glad when I saw that the officer who was on duty then was a Christian and as he walked over he asked what was wrong. I told him all that had happened and afterwards he said, "Let me pray for you." I was glad he did. I had lost my peace for a while, but now it returned.

"Don't give up on me, God hasn't finished with me yet!"

Christians are not sinless; they just sin less. I am glad to say that was the only time that I can recall when, as a believer in prison, I lost my witness. It takes years to build it up and only a minute to lose it. As I often say, "Don't give up on me, God hasn't finished with me yet!"

I have always enjoyed reading; it's a way of escape for many men in prison and there are certain classics that are read by almost everyone. Books like *The Godfather, Exodus,* and *Papillion.* One such book for me was *The Cross & the Switchblade* which tells the story of how an organisation called Teen Challenge was begun by a man called David Wilkerson. It tells of the conversion of Nicky Cruz who was a gang leader from the streets of New York. I was greatly touched by reading it and thought I would love to be involved in a work like this. To watch God working in the lives of broken people and making them whole. This was what He was doing in my own life. (I never imagined I would meet this guy several years later, and his daughter would come and stay with us in Belfast for six months).

It was a real surprise to find a postal address of Teen Challenge in Northern Ireland on the back cover of this book. I was so touched by this work I decided to send them a small donation, so I saved up some of my wages for a few weeks (at that time we got paid the grand sum of £2.50 a week) and I sent it off to them. They sent me a nice letter back and thanked me and said they would remember me in their prayers. I never thought much more about it.

"You sent Teen Challenge a donation about five years ago."

Almost six years later, I wasn't long released from prison, when one day I was introduced to this Pastor called Roy Kerr. As soon as I told him my name he immediately said to me, "You sent Teen Challenge a donation about five years ago." He was the Director of Teen Challenge in Northern Ireland. I was overwhelmed. We had only just met, yet when he heard my name he remembered my letter. We became good friends after that. He was the man who introduced me to the ministry of Teen Challenge, and got me personally involved in the work. I always love to be in this man's company: he has this gift to make you feel as if you are important. He is a real 'Barnabas' – an encourager if ever there was one. He would never let you leave without praying for you first. I would always come away as if I were walking ten foot tall.

There were some funny times too. Once when I was working down in the kitchen, I was frying the bread and started talking to another prisoner telling him about how real God can be. I got so carried away I forgot to lift the bread out of the deep fat fryers! There was black smoke billowing everywhere!

When the screw walked across to me, I thought, *I am in trouble now*. He looked down and saw the Bible in my hand and said, "I know, I know, man shall not live by bread alone." He just turned and walked away.

It was eighteen months later I read in the Bible about new Christians being baptised in water. I kept coming across references to being baptised, and the thought came to me: *That's what I need to do, to get baptised in water!* The thought stayed with me for weeks, and one day while working in the kitchen I was thinking about this; it happened the Governor was doing his rounds and was in the kitchen at that particular time. As he was passing me I spoke up and said, "Sir may I speak with you a moment?"

He stopped dead, and his two escort officers looked at me in disbelief. It was against all the prison regulations to do such a thing. I did it on the spur of the moment – it certainly wasn't planned. I even surprised myself by doing such a thing. The Governor looked at me and said, "This is highly irregular, Hamilton, if you wish to speak to me you put in a request in to do so!"

I quickly tried to apologise, "I am sorry Sir..." but before I got a chance to finish, he said "What is it you want?" I went on to tell him I was a Christian and I felt it was important for me to be obedient to the command of Christ to be baptised. He surprised me by saying it was certainly right to do so (I found out he was actually an ordained Baptist minister.) Then he asked next, "You are not hoping to get released to do this, are you Hamilton?" I laughed, and said, "I cannot see that happening Sir..." He came back to me and said, "Well where do you suggest we hold this baptismal service?" I quickly replied, "In the bath-house Sir!" He looked at me for a moment and answered, "Leave it with me I will think about it," and off he went. Of course everyone was standing watching all this, and one of the officers said, "Hamilton, you're lucky, if anyone else tried that, they would find themselves on the Boards, but not you! You must have someone up there on your side!" I had to laugh, "It certainly wasn't my idea, believe me!"

It must have been a month later; I hadn't heard a word back, then out of the blue, I was called down to see the Gov. He told me it was all planned. I was overjoyed! "Are there any others besides you?" he asked. By this time I had asked a number of guys if they wanted to be baptised if we could get permission. There were another five guys who had got saved and wanted to go through the waters of baptism. So I gave the Governor their names!

A week later while everyone else was locked up, our cell-doors were opened and we were given a new towel and a new pair of underpants and told to go down to the bathhouse. It was amazing, all the officers on duty at that time were Christians!

We had tried our best for it to be kept secret, but everyone knew. As we tried to tiptoe down the landing, guys started to bang their doors and shout things out! "Davey walks on water!" My face was turning bright red by this time, and we were all practically running now just to get out of the wing and to get away from all the banter. The whole jail knew what was happening! It was the talk for days!

Down in the bath-house we filled a bath up with lukewarm water, we were a little nervous by it all; really none of us prisoners knew what to do, so I said, "Just follow me guys, do whatever I do!"

I climbed into the bath, and was told by the minister to slide up until my knees were almost touching the huge taps. After making a confession of faith to the minister, (who had been invited into the prison to conduct this baptismal service) he prayed as he bent me backwards under the water and lifted me up again. It was fantastic! Everyone was laughing and smiling, even the Governor (highly irregular!)

The whole jail knew what was happening! It was the talk for days!

All five other candidates followed me, and the last particular guy was a big guy called Geordie and he was massive. When Geordie climbed in and lay back the water just rushed up the sides of the bath and soaked everybody standing at the side of the bath watching. Every one of them looked at the Governor to see his reaction; the front of his suit was dripping wet! The Governor looked down at his jacket and turned and looked at the guy's jacket standing beside him and then he burst out laughing. Only then did the others feel free to join in too!

After they refilled the bath Big Geordie eventually got baptised too. So it's on official record, as far as I am aware, that the first baptismal service in Belfast Prison was on the 29th of May 1981. I know others have taken place since but not officially; it's usually the inmates who do it by themselves, without any official involvement.

I was still doing the leather work in partnership with my mate Big J. One day we had a row, because a man ordered some items and promised to pay me the day he got released. I decided to trust him but he failed to come across with the money. Of course Big J was furious. He said it was my fault we had lost thirty pounds because I was a Christian now and trusted everybody and now we were being ripped off. He made a new rule: from now on, no one gets anything unless they pay first, money up front!

"As a Christian I want to look for the good in people not the bad."

"No more trusting people OK?"

"I cannot agree to that," I answered back. "As a Christian I want to look for the good in people not the bad; I want people to see I trust them."

"You and your trust, what about our thirty pounds?!" he shouted back.

"Listen" I said, "You haven't lost any money; it's my loss OK?"

"You're mad, Davey, since you have become a Christian, do you know that?"

I laughed, "Do you think so?" he shook his head and off he went.

As I was lying on my bed I thought about our conversation, and I said to the Lord, "I think it's right to trust people. I don't like this thing of saying I don't trust you so you must pay up front. Lord show me if I am doing the right thing."

He answered me in an unusual way. It was a few days later, I got my weekly visit from my mother. During the course of our conversation she said to me, "David, something strange happened the other night, this man who lives near us, who is a Christian, called to our house on Friday night, and said, 'I know this may sound strange to you Mrs Hamilton, but I was praying earlier and this thought came into my head to give your son David thirty pounds. I believe it was God who told me to do this, so will you accept it please and leave it for him? Tell him it's from the Lord."

I could not believe what I was hearing! "Mum, wait till you hear the story behind it," I said. She was amazed by it all. Of course after my visit that day the first person I wanted to tell was my mate Big J. When I found him, he was playing a game of snooker, so I called him over to tell him. "Wait till you hear this! You will not believe it," I said. When I told him the whole story he just stood there motionless. At the end he said, "Is that it? That would have been sixty pounds we would have had, if you hadn't had trusted your man."

He was completely blinded to the fact that God had worked a miracle!

The man who God used to replace the thirty pounds I had lost was Derek Jackson, an ex-terrorist who had been miraculously healed of cancer.

Derek began to visit me after that. He would write and send me in study books which helped me a lot in my early days. When I got out on my first parole he took me to my first Christian meeting on the outside. I have never seen this man without a smile on his face; he always seems to radiate the Lord. He was another of those special people that God sent alongside me to build me up in my own walk.

That experience helped me a lot to believe God for miracles, to pray for miracles, and to see miracles take place. Another time I remember it was coming in to the winter nights, and it was starting to get cold out in the exercise yard. I needed a jacket to keep me warm, so I prayed and asked the Lord to help me get a denim jacket – not a Wrangler, which were the most popular at that time, but instead I wanted a Levi jacket. It was the following day a guy came into my cell and said, "My mother! I asked her to get me a denim jacket and send it in, what does she buy me? A Levi, and I told her a Wrangler. It's even the wrong size for me; it's too big; she cannot do anything right." My curiosity was stirred, "What size is the jacket?" I asked. "42," he answered. "Why, are you interested in buying it? It's going cheap."

He asked for six ounces of tobacco. I said no, "I'll give you ten, OK?" He couldn't believe his luck. I always had loads of tobacco, so it was no problem to pay him. I was thrilled to have a new Levi denim jacket so soon, and my friend was just as thrilled to get rid of it so quickly.

I knew it was God's provision in answer to prayer.

Chapter Twelve

THE HUNGER STRIKE

I became a Christian at the start of the year 1980 and the Republican hunger strike began in October the same year. Seven Republican prisoners in the H-blocks began a hunger strike. The British government appeared to concede the prisoners' right to wear their own clothes. The strike was called off in December before any prisoners died. We thought we would be allowed to wear our own clothes again. But it soon emerged that the British government were simply intending to give the prisoners the right to wear civilian-style clothing supplied by the prison, and had duped the hunger strikers into ending it.

That's what happened, we were issued with civilian-style clothing – when we saw these we were disgusted. I received a pair of grey slacks and a pink and white striped shirt and a pillar box red jumper to wear, and black high heel shoes. What a let-down. The old grey prison denim garb looked far better.

Early in the new year, 1981, we found out a second hunger strike had begun. It was led by Bobby Sands, one of my former mates from Rathcoole; he himself was the first to refuse food. He was the new IRA Commanding Officer in the H-blocks. It began to hit the news outside. The political atmosphere outside the prisons became electric, even in the South of Ireland. It resulted in widespread rioting in all the nationalist areas in the North of Ireland.

Shortly after the hunger strike began, the independent Irish Republican MP for Fermanagh & South Tyrone died and Bobby Sands was nominated as a candidate, he was elected as the new MP in April that year. Three weeks later, in May 1981 he died from his self-imposed fast in the prison hospital.

Our group of Christians in the prison, like many Christians all around the world, were praying that God would intervene. The prison Chaplain during a Sunday morning service suggested we should pray about the hunger strike situation. He no sooner spoke the words and all the Loyalists were ordered out of the service. "We will not be praying for no hunger strikers," they shouted out. With that they all arose and marched back to their wings.

There was nothing for me. I was told the reason was I was praying for the hunger strikers.

There was only a small number of men who remained; I was one of them. A few days later when I was at work in the prison laundry I decided to have a time of prayer. I used the drying room for my private place of prayer. Because it was like a sauna room no one liked to go into it. I would sit in there for ten minutes and pray away, out loud even. While I was doing this, another prisoner came in, but I didn't see him. I was behind all these sheets that where hung up to dry. At the break time that morning I went over to collect my tea and sandwiches as usual. But there was nothing for me. I was told the reason was I was praying for the hunger strikers, so I could join them on hunger strike too, because I was getting nothing from now on. This treatment lasted until the hunger strike ended.

I remember how it ended: the announcement of Bobby's death prompted several days of riots in nationalist areas of Northern Ireland. That next morning, a Protestant man and his son were delivering milk in a nationalist area in Belfast and they were stoned to death by an angry crowd. Both he and his young son died in retaliation for Bobby's death. What was ironic was that I knew all three of them – like Bobby, they had also come from Rathcoole.

Over the ensuing months, nine more hunger strikers died. In late summer, the hunger strike began to weaken, in a large part due to the actions of a radical Roman Catholic priest, Fr. Denis Faul, who boldly intervened with hunger strikers' families to urge them to give consent to the prison authorities for their relatives to be fed by drip after they had lost consciousness. The first prisoner whose family intervened was Paddy Quinn. Again this happened with a number of other prisoners' families who had decided that their relative's death would be futile.

One of those men who participated was Liam McCloskey, an INLA member, who joined the hunger strike on 3 August 1981 and ended the strike on 26 September 1981 after 55 days without food. When it became known to him that his family would intervene to save his life after he became unconscious, he made the decision himself to end it then. Just a week later, on 3 October 1981, the IRA and INLA leadership called off the hunger strike. Liam also made a decision to accept Christ and became a committed Christian from that time on.

Both Liam and I got released from prison around the same time, Christmas 1983. I attended a Prison Fellowship rally at that time and James McIlroy introduced us to each other. We began doing a lot of meetings together, all around the province. It got a lot of publicity, two former terrorists from opposite sides of the community now spending much of our time involved in cross-community work. We started going into schools and colleges and speaking to students from both sides of the divide. We were asked by Scripture Union if we would make a documentary video of each of our stories that could be used in schools. This we did and it became a great success. (It was called 'Under the Shadow.') The Northern Ireland Education and Library Board then approached us to make an educational video for classroom use, again this we did and it is currently used in schools as part of the revised curriculum.

One of my close friends who was in prison with me was a guy called Artie Beck. He was well known in Loyalist circles and well-liked by all who knew him. He was hilarious, a real character always playing jokes and messing around. He was known to us as 'Big Artie.' He was around the 6' mark, but while in prison he took an illness called osteoporosis. His spine began to crumble and he started to shrink. At the start the prison medical authorities took no notice as he sought help about his condition; eventually as he got smaller, it became noticeable to everyone. It was only then he began to get some treatment, but by then it was too late, the osteoporosis eventually killed him. Big Artie was less than 5' foot when he died.

Artie happened to be in the hospital wing at the time all this was happening with the hunger strikers. He later shared a story with me that is worth relating about an incident that he witnessed. There was an old lady who was a prison visitor. She was well known around the prison, to staff and prisoners alike. She would walk around the wings and talk to the prisoners. She always had comic tracts of a Christian nature to give out to those who would accept them. They were read by nearly everyone, even the hunger strikers. This old lady actually came in to the Maze on Christmas day and do the rounds and if she came across a prisoner who had no Christmas cards in his cell, she would write one out and hand it to him. Artie told me one day while she was over at the hospital block, he was in the big ward where there were five or six beds, there with the hunger strikers. As this old lady walked around the beds she offered out the tracts. One of the hunger strikers was looking at the tracts and said, "I've read that one," so she exchanged it for another, again he said, "I've read that one as well," so she offered him another, again he did the same thing three or four times.

Next thing he give out a loud cry, and everyone looked over to see what it was about.

"I have no more," she said.

"Have you anything else I can read?" he asked.

"All I have is this," she replied, and she produced a comic book A4 size from her white cloth carrier bag. It was some of the New Testament stories in the same format. He accepted it. Not long afterwards she left them. It was later that evening this hunger striker was lying on his bed reading this book. Next thing he give out a loud cry, and everyone looked over to see what it was about. He turned the comic book around and pointed to a picture and said to them all, "That's me about to go under!" He was pointing at a picture of St Peter in the sea with his hands outstretched and the waves just below his head, it had the words of Peter crying out to Jesus, "Lord save me!" As this poor man read these words he cried out himself, "Lord save me too!" I was overwhelmed when Artie told me this story. It was not long after this, I believe, that this hunger striker died too.

I sincerely believe that that hunger striker called out to the Lord Jesus Christ, and God answered his prayer and he is in glory with Him now. I like how the hymn writer puts it:

The vilest offender who truly believes
That moment from Jesus a pardon receives.

I don't think any of the hunger strikers could have ever imagined in their wildest dreams what would actually be accomplished by their sacrifice. When they began their protest, it was seen as just another protest that would not accomplish any real change. It didn't even have the support of many Republicans outside; it was their personal fight, apart from those who were related to somebody in the prison. (Known as RACs, those who did support the hunger strikers were very much in the minority, they had to fight long and hard to get them any real support.) I think the lack of the support was due to the fact that many nationalists concluded that if it failed, like other hunger strikes before, it would do so much damage for the Republican cause outside. For Sinn Fein it was not really their main issue. They needed to be more focused, other things needed their attention. They could ill afford to take the chance of actually getting involved with it or really be behind it. I wonder in all honesty how many of them could truly have seen what this hunger strike would achieve for them. The British government throughout the seventies had tried to bring politicians from both sides of the divide together in an effort to find a solution, all of which ended in failure. As they moved into the 1980s the situation was bleak, with no apparent hope of a resolution being found. In 1981 Mrs Thatcher as Prime Minister was determined to break the IRA; they believed through these Republican hunger-strikes they could demoralize the IRA once and for all, and now was the right time to strike. No compromise.

Yet I believe that this hunger strike played a major role in preparing the way for the peace process. To me, looking back then, I think the hunger strike event was the catalyst within the militant Republican movement that brought significant changes from the early 1980s onwards.

> *I believe that this hunger strike played a major role in preparing the way for the peace process.*

Within the Republican movement in the H-blocks there was an internal debate as to the sustainability of the conflict outside; some were beginning to question the "long war" strategy designed to wear the British down. Was it right to continue with the bullet and the bomb? Perhaps there could be another way a more political approach. This was confirmed and achieved by Bobby Sands being elected MP for Fermanagh-South Tyrone. From POW to politician, who could believe such a tiny hinge could swing open such a mighty door?

This was the impetus needed to move towards a more political agenda, not long afterwards there emerged other new leaders which culminated with the election of Gerry Adams as President of Sinn Fein (SF) in 1983. This was followed soon after with the start of talks between himself and John Hume, the leader of the nationalist Social Democratic and Labour Party (SDLP). In turn this led to a number of pro-nationalists forming a coalition that eventually led to the Downing Street Declaration signed by the British Prime Minister John Major and the Taoiseach Albert Reynolds in 1993. The following year this political approach was echoed by the Protestant paramilitary groups. The Progressive Unionist Party (PUP) and the Ulster Democratic Party (UDP) representing the political wings of the UVF and UDA portrayed a willingness to meet around the table, something still lacking in the constitutional Unionist parties.

Since then we have seen the Good Friday Agreement; some will argue it was broken by the IRA bomb in Canary Wharf in 1996. But progress since then has admittedly been rather slow and there have been major setbacks, even with several suspended devolved institutions starting and stopping, no one is naive enough to think we can find a political solution in the near future which will be acceptable to all. Yet despite this we have since seen the demilitarisation by all sides which has brought an air of normality and calm back to the streets of Northern Ireland. The peace process has delivered change we could never have envisaged in 1994. Despite these successes we know there are still a number of obstacles remaining. But we have so much to be thankful for.

Today the Crumlin Road Gaol and HMP The Maze (H-blocks)

are no longer in use, gone and forgotten by all accounts, except perhaps, in the minds of those who endured its harsh regime. Many still carry the mental scars and sadly, for others, the trauma of the Northern Ireland conflict still lives on to haunt the present.

Chapter Thirteen

THE OLD MAN AND THE NEW MAN

For every young Christian there is always a crisis that seems to follow conversion. The devil doesn't like to let anyone go without a fight. He will try everything to bring you back to himself. He knows where to hit to hurt you, and where it will hurt the most. He hit me hard, and I mean hard!

I wasn't long a Christian when I found out that my wife actually had another man living in our home with her. This was a terrible shock to me. I could not believe it especially as she was still coming up to visit me each week. The friend who told me thought I already knew about this because apparently this other man had moved into my home a few months before. This is the biggest fear for any married man in prison. What I had always feared was now happening to me!

The next eight months I did everything to try to save my marriage but to no avail. During that period there were times I got my hopes up only to see them dashed again. Once I got a letter suggesting we could make a go of it. I was so happy when I read this, but it was short lived. The final straw for me happened when I was moved up to a new cell on the top landing. From there, out of my new cell window I could look down to the street and watch people coming in and out of the prison. I could wave to my family and friends as they were getting into their cars. On my first visit with my wife since moving cells, we sat and held hands and kissed throughout the visit. Afterwards I thought, *I will surprise her by shouting out my cell window and waving to her as she crosses the road to go home.* I rushed back to my cell, climbed up and waited for her to leave the prison.

After a few minutes I saw her crossing the road and walking towards her car. As I took a deep breath to shout, her car door opened and a man got out and he kissed her. My legs started to shake; my stomach knotted. I felt as if I had been gutted as I watched them drive away. While my wife had been sitting holding my hand across the table telling me how much she loved me, outside the prison another man was sitting waiting to take her home. She had told me she had finished with this man a month ago and wanted to save our marriage and I was so happy. But when with my own eyes I saw them together, I knew it was all lies; nothing had changed in their relationship.

That day I knew my marriage was over, it was only all a dream.

That day I knew my marriage was over; it was only all a dream. I had to accept the hard facts: I no longer had a wife. Furthermore, I had lost my son and he was calling another man Daddy. During an earlier visit he actually said to me, I have two daddies now, and I realised then what the child had meant. I had no home to go back to. I found it hard to sleep and – worse – when I did, it was only to wake up with this terrible gut feeling of loneliness. It was hard to hide the pain, and yet I knew God would have to do something inside of me. I couldn't really share my hurt with anyone. I tried to, with a few other Christians, but they couldn't really understand what was happening. They all came out with these 'holy hallowed' clichés: "Praise God, you're better off without her," or, "All things work for our good, trust God."

I realised they meant good, but that wasn't what I wanted to hear. It wasn't healing the hurt in my heart. I needed someone to put their arm around me and just be a shoulder to cry on. Sadly you don't find such people in prison. I only had God to turn to, but at times I felt my prayers stopped at the ceiling. This time of depression lasted almost a year. I realised loneliness is not not being loved, because my family loved me and wrote letters to me, but rather loneliness is not having someone to love, to care for.

It is in all of us – the need to be needed, to be wanted and loved by others. I continued to pray and ask God to heal my heart and to remove the love I still had for my wife. Eventually through much prayer and fasting I later filed for a divorce, after having read everything in the Bible about the subject. Again I got mixed reactions from some of my Christian friends in prison. Some said divorce was a sin: period. Others pointed out that God divorced the Northern Kingdom of Israel for her adulterous ways. All I knew was I did not want a divorce but that's what happened – it was part of the sentence. It didn't get any easier after that; God still had much to do to make my healing complete. I knew He would have to do something inside of me to relieve my broken heart. I just had to trust and leave everything with Him.

The devil didn't let up on me either. The hardest test of all was when this man and my wife had a row and in anger he hit my five-year-old son in the face and broke his nose. My son went into hospital and had an operation on his nose, but the bone structure was completely shattered and he had to wait for the bone to develop before they could fix it. He developed a stutter and sometimes he would wake up screaming in the middle of the night because he couldn't breathe. It was my sister who told me what had happened to my boy.

I couldn't believe this! Who would do such a thing to a small child? I was very upset and angry, mostly at myself, for not being there to protect my son. I began to pray about this man, and I told God if he came into jail I would stop being a Christian and kill him: he didn't deserve to live. Any time he came into my mind I would pray "God keep him out of jail, out of my way."

It was three years later when I got out on my parole. Everyone who knew the story told me not to go near my ex-wife (by this time she was living with someone else) or to go looking for this man. I didn't have any plans, but I wanted to see my boy, which I did, but I never saw this particular man. I wasn't worried about it, I knew I would eventually meet him, but I didn't expect to meet him so soon in the way that I did!

My parole ended and I went back into prison. I walked up and put my brown paper bag on top of my bed, lifted my cup and turned to go out and get some hot water for a cup of tea. I saw a man on the other landing looking over at me. It was him! He had come into jail during the time I went home on parole. My heart started to beat faster. He immediately pulled his cell door closed, which automatically locks it. He stayed locked and refused to come out.

I knew he would have to come out some time and I would be ready for him when he did.

A few days later I was cutting the grass at the prison hospital. I was standing at the path and happened to look up and saw this man walking towards me, escorted by an officer over to the hospital. When he saw me he stopped and then walked around to the other side of the officer, so he was now between us. When he came to where I was, I said to him, "Have you punched any babies lately?" He replied, "It was an accident."

"You are a Christian and you just said you are going to kill that man."

"I am going to kill you." I answered.

The officer told him to keep on walking and just stared at me. There was a guy working along with me and he couldn't believe what I had just said to this man.

"You are a Christian and you just said you are going to kill that man."

"You don't know what he did to my son," was my answer to him.

During lock-up after lunch I would usually read my Bible and pray. I would look out the hatch of my door to see if he had come out for exercise. For a few weeks he remained locked, but then one day he decided to go outside. I watched as he walked downstairs I decided to prepare myself. I began to walk up and down my cell I wanted to get rid of my other emotions, to feel nothing but the desire to kill this man. I knew the yard was the best place to do what I had planned to do, I had to block out everything else and not worry about an officer seeing me. There was a distraction I had organised for this event to draw the screws away. If all went according to plan, it would be all over in a few moments; a body would be lying in the yard and the sirens would go off. There was little possibility of my being caught. I saw it happen before and no one was charged with the murder.

It would be all over in a few moments; a body would be lying in the yard and the sirens would go off.

I was walking up and down waiting for the door to open, and waiting for the urge to raise up inside me to want to kill him. I was finding it hard – I couldn't seem to do it, there was no evil in me. I was struggling and feeling frustration, it was then God spoke to me in my mind, "David, forgive him." I answered back, "I'll forgive him after I've killed him," and I kept walking. Again it happened that I had this thought, "David, forgive him," so I said, " I will not kill him, but I want to beat him badly, for it's only right to do this, he deserves it."

I wanted to make a deal with God, and God didn't want to know. All I could hear was "David, forgive him." So I got angry with God, stopped walking, looked up and shouted, "Look what he did to my son!" It was then God spoke to me again and said, "Look what they did to my Son!"

I fell to my knees and wept and I asked God to help me forgive him. I came up from my knees a different man. I went out into the yard where I saw him standing under the shelter. He was afraid – he reminded me of a scared rabbit caught in car headlights. As I walked towards him he did not move. I stopped just a few feet from him. I looked in his eyes and saw the fear. I could easily have taken his life at that moment. Instead I said, "I am a Christian now. God has forgiven me and I forgive you for what you did to my son. You can stay in the yard; no one will harm you." I walked back inside to my cell and lay down; I couldn't believe what I had just done.

It was a few days later I was called for a visit – my mother was up to see me, this man was called on a visit also. On our way down to the visiting area we had to go together through an 'air lock.' You go through a steel gate and you are locked in, when you walk to the other end then a screw opens another gate to let you pass through. The moment we were locked in this area he assumed I would attack him and he squatted down onto the floor trying to cover his face with his hands. I told him to get up. "I am not going to touch you," I said, and I turned and walked away.

As I sat talking to my mother, I saw his mother get up and come across to my table. I stood up to meet her, and she actually put her arms around me and thanked me for forgiving her son. I didn't know what to say back to her so I said, "I am a Christian now," and she smiled and went back to her seat. Later on back in the cell I was lying on my bed thinking about what had happened. I still found it hard to believe I actually let him go – I had stabbed other people for less; I had beaten other guys with hammers for less. As I lay there, suddenly a thought ran across my mind, it was this, *I REALLY am a Christian. I REALLY am a Christian!*

Where did the evil go from within me? Who took it away? –

God!

Where did the forgiveness come from? Who gave me this? –
God!

It was God!

That day was a turning point in my life. I knew then I would
never go back to my old life, or back to the organisation
again. I would never hold a gun or plant another bomb as
long as I would live. From that day on I have never doubted
my salvation because I know the power of God to change a
person. Just as it says in the Bible, in 2 Corinthians 5 verse
17: "if any man be in Christ, he is a new creature: old things
are passed away; behold, all things are become new."

Chapter Fourteen

DAVEY THE PREACHER

"It's all right for these guys coming in here telling us how God can change our lives; they go back out again. If I was going with them I'd be smiling too."

I was sitting directly behind the guy who made this comment during the Methodist service in church one Thursday afternoon. I thought, *It's difficult to get any message across to these men because they cannot relate to them, so no one gives a thought to what they have to say.* The thought came into my mind, *they would listen to me because I don't get to go home afterwards. I also go back to my cell.* Perhaps I should talk to them and share my own experience of how my life has changed since becoming a Christian a few months earlier.

For some reason this thought remained with me, several times over the next week – You speak to them. I laughed to myself, No way – I'd make a complete fool of myself. Anyway the boys would give me a death; they would be shouting out things, maybe even throw the hymnbooks at me. I couldn't see myself standing up at the front speaking to all these guys. Yet the thought still stayed with me. It continued for another week, then I had another thought, maybe this is God talking to me. I had heard many Christians say things like that, "Then God said to me... " I always wondered how they knew it was God speaking to them. How does God speak to people? Is it an audible voice, or what? Now I was a little confused, was this God telling me to do this? I think being Irish it takes things a little longer to reach the brain: *What if it is God?* Man, that means I have to do it! Now I was a nervous wreck!

I decided I would have to fast to check it out, and if it was God's idea, He would have to get the prison chaplain to agree to it. That would be one way of proving it; he would have to allow me to get up to talk, as far as I was aware no other prisoner had ever done this before. The chaplain would be taking a chance: he wouldn't know what I would do. When I told him what was on my mind he asked me what I planned to say to them; I really didn't know. "I just want to tell them that God has changed my life," that was all I could tell him. I was sort of expecting him to say "No, maybe some other time," but when he said, "OK, in a fortnight's time you can speak on the Sunday morning," I almost died! Now I had really done it, he had said yes! Oh no!

"I just want to tell them that God has changed my life,"

The next two weeks were the longest I spent in jail! I fasted for three days during that first week seeking God to give me the words to speak. The next week I did the same again. I prayed and asked God to confirm it as well by letting someone get converted by my testimony; that was the only thing I wanted in return. It had been announced the Sunday before that the speaker for the following week would be a Mr David Hamilton coming all the way from 'D' Wing. Of course it was the talk of the jail. Guys were shouting things at me all week like, "Davey, will you be dressing up like Batman on Sunday morning?" or, "You're only doing this so you can get at the wine in the minister's room!" It was never said in a hostile way, always as a laugh. But man was I nervous!

Finally Sunday came around. I have never seen the church as full, and some of the guys there hadn't been in church since they were christened as babies! I was out in the back room with the Rev David Jardine – he wanted us to pray before the service began, I remember he asked me, "Are you all set? Have you got your notes ready?"

"No, I don't have any."

"What are you going to say to them?" was his next question.

I looked at him with a slight smile, or perhaps it was more of a nervous gesture than anything else and said, "I don't know, but God knows." I think I saw the same look on his own face before he said, "Let's go out and join the others."

I tried to avoid making eye contact with anyone; I found it hard to sing the hymns and I could sense everyone looking at me. Occasionally I would glance quickly over all the faces in the congregation, and immediately regret doing so.

It seemed like the service had gone on for four hours, and yet before I knew it, it was my turn next, when the minister said, "Our speaker needs no introduction today. Most of you know him, it's David Hamilton, all the way from 'D' wing."

The whole place erupted with shouts and whistles; my face was as red as a beetroot! I just stood there motionless, waiting for it to die down. Many times I had taken part in this very thing, now here I was at the receiving end! Now I knew how some of those speakers must have felt. After a minute or two the place settled, and I began to talk to them. One guy who was a well-known leader of a Terrorist group, shouted out, "Davey, you haven't repented of everything you did!" Again there was an outburst of laughter. "Maybe not to the police, but to God I have, so that's enough for me!" I shouted back. Again everyone laughed. I now was beginning to relax; it seemed all the nervousness I had just a few minutes before was completely gone – it was replaced with boldness and a confidence. Now I had no fear at all! I just began to tell them the truth that my life was completely changed since I had asked Jesus to take charge of my life a year before. I told them it was the best year of my life, (that got quite a few laughs) and yet in another way it was also the hardest year of my life. Some of them who were my friends outside were aware of my domestic problems – at that particular time I was still praying for reconciliation to take place with my wife. I told them that through it all I had someone who stuck closer to me than a friend, and that He was interested as much in them as He was in me, and that person was the Lord Jesus Christ.

It seemed the bolder I got the quieter they got! I knew God was moving amongst them by the power of the Holy Spirit. That day was a turning point in my life. From then on, the only desire I had was to tell people that Jesus loved them and could change their lives as he changed mine. Nothing excites me more; even today, I still feel exactly the same, I have no real care for anything else. Before that day, I would have said I was introverted, timid in the fear of making a fool of myself. I hadn't any great education, so I had no confidence in doing something outside the group; I had what is known as a 'gang-set mentality', yet that day I realised I had stepped out from it and had begun to stand alone. I was making my own decisions now. Afterwards I talked with the chaplain. He told me he couldn't believe how long I had spoken for, and without the use of any notes. I knew God had anointed me; it was as if He had taken over and put the words in my mouth, as He promises in His Word.

What I didn't know then was that the anointing that day would be confirmed to me not so far in the future, and that I would become an evangelist and that would be my work full-time.

Neither the chaplain or I could have imagined then that that event would be the first of many times when we would share the platform together. Nor would it be confined to this particular

I knew God had anointed me; it was as if He had taken over and put the words in my mouth.

prison, or indeed to Northern Ireland, but that we would find ourselves doing the same thing again in prisons and churches around New York, USA!

The next few days following the service I was waiting to hear if anyone had made a decision to follow Christ. Thursday came – still nothing. I went to the Methodist Church service that afternoon. When the minister, Rev Robert Russell (in prison there was a chaplain for each of the four main denominations; Presbyterian, Anglican, Methodist and Roman Catholic) got up to preach he said, "I want to tell you men something that happened on Sunday night past." He went on to say how he had challenged his congregation that evening by telling them that a young man who got converted in the prison, a year before, was the preacher that morning in the jail, standing up to witness before all those men how God had changed his life. "That takes guts! how many of you could do it?" he asked. "How many of you are willing to stand up now and acknowledge you need God in your life?"

He followed on by saying that it was only a few moments later that an old lady stood up and made her way out to the centre aisle and slowly walked to the front of the church. She told him she had been coming to church sixty years and never once had made a commitment of her life to Christ. She said, "That young man, even though he's in prison has something in his life that I lack. I want to know God in the way that he does." When I heard this I couldn't stop the tears from flowing. Someone had got saved from hearing my testimony, but not in the way I expected, not a prisoner, but an old lady over seventy years old!

Someone had got saved from hearing my testimony, but not in the way I expected.

Later on, I made a vow to God that I would never speak to a stranger for more than three minutes without telling him how God had changed my life. I have sought to live by that same vow for the past seventeen years now. And do you know something else? It still excites me even now when I share the Gospel – it's the greatest message known to man.

The last two years of my sentence was spent working up in the prison garden. My job was cutting the grass, this took me all over the prison working. We had a prison grave-yard, where prisoners who were hung got buried. It was a patch of land behind the prison hospital, alongside the high stone wall, and was used by the dog handlers as a run to exercise their dogs in. It was always a gloomy place to work, it seemed the sun never reached into this particular corner. There was nothing to suggest it was actually a cemetery. The nearest clue to be found was on the cold stone wall, where at eye level you could see etched out on one of the stones a name and a date. That was all and even this was crudely done so that one would think it to be no different from a thousand other names found scraped on the prison walls all around the place. But I knew the difference. Most men who etched their names out wrote their name and how long their sentence was, but for those buried there it was just the date they were executed, and it was carved by someone else. The only good thing about working in that little graveyard was the peace and quietness that I often experienced there. It was perhaps the only place in the whole jail I could actually get to be alone with the Lord.

I have a Bible with around fifty autographs signed on the back pages, mostly signatures of men who were doing time with me, or of special speakers. One of the special memories that is reflected by those autographs is that of the prison chaplain Rev Bill Vance. He had been off work for a long time recovering from major heart surgery, but returned one Thursday night to lead our Bible study group. I was pleased to see him and remained to talk to him after the others had left, just for five minutes before lock-up. He always had a smile, never once did I hear him complain or talk harshly about any one. If I complained about how I felt I had been mistreated by an officer, Bill would answer, "We should pray for him; we don't know what's going on in his life or what concerns are causing him to act that way." That's what we would end up doing, praying. That night before I went to lock up, I asked him to sign my Bible for me which he did. He wrote a reference as well, which I never stopped to read then, for I could hear doors slamming shut and I was already late for lock up. So I said, "Have to run here, goodnight Bill!" I remember he looked up with that familiar smile, and answered "Goodnight," as he lifted his hand and waved as I ran out the door.

The following morning, I went down to my work, as soon as I walked in, an officer called me over and said, "I've some bad news for you, David – the Rev Vance died early this morning." I could hardly take it in; I was very upset. I found it hard to work, so the officer allowed me to go back to my cell. The first thing I did was to lift my Bible and see what Bill had written, the night before. His words pierced my heart: "For I am persuaded, that neither death, nor life, nor angels, nor principalities, nor powers, nor things present, nor things to come, nor height, nor depth, nor any other created thing shall be able to separate us from the love of God, which is in Christ Jesus our Lord." (Romans 8:38) I smiled to myself, and thought, Bill Vance was ready to go; he wasn't afraid to die, because he knew Jesus personally. That's why he could write that precious text in my Bible.

Another is the signature of a prison officer I have fond memories of. One day while I working up the garden, I was standing at the wire fence talking to him. I knew him to be a fine Christian, he was probably the most respected officer in 'the Crum'. He was one of the gym instructors. There were two officers who were responsible for all the physical fitness in the prison, and they were as different as chalk and cheese.

The other guy liked to be seen as a tough guy – he was a big guy for sure. He enjoyed getting the chance to beat prisoners up: he was on the riot squad and loved it! I remembered him from the riot we had in 'C' Wing a few years before. He was fond of a drink but if he got too much, we got no exercise in the gym. If he was working on the Saturday we never knew for certain if we would get a football match; if he had had the night out, then he would most probably forget about having a match. But Sam was totally the opposite, he would go out of his way to make sure the guys got their football, even to the extent of coming into work during his holidays. Sam was up cutting the grass verge around the edge of the pitch, using diesel to burn away the weeds. Between us was this seven-metre-high fence topped with razor wire. After we had talked for a while I turned to go back to my work and he turned around to carry on with his. I hadn't walked fifteen metres away when I heard a massive explosion behind me, and I turned around to see a huge black mushroom shaped cloud raising upwards. As the smoke cleared I could hardly believe my eyes! He was standing there burning in front of me: all of his clothes were burned off, I could not go to help him. I cursed that high fence and ran up to the office and shouted to the officer to sound the alarm. Before he lifted the phone, the alarm sounded – the sound of the explosion had been heard all over the prison and naturally they all assumed it was a terrorist attack. I ran back to the fence where other prisoners were gathered watching the drama. By this time another officer was on hand and he was rolling "Jaunty" (that's what we called him) across the ground to put out the fire. Parts of his flesh were still burning. The officer was one of the dog handlers on patrol around the perimeter so he happened to be quite close by when the explosion happened and it was he that sounded the alarm. He immediately ran to his aid.

Of course, all the men who were Christians were praying for his recovery.

Later on we were told his heart stopped on the way to hospital. Apparently this happened three times, but they were able to bring him back, thanks to the medics. It was touch and go if he would live, he had multiple body burns. Of course all the men who were Christians were praying for his recovery, and many others besides, I was amazed how many other prisoners said to me, "Don't forget to pray for Jaunty." I was not surprised to find out that the tuck shop was sold out of 'get well' cards, bought by prisoners to send to this officer! "Why?" was the question many officers were asking; what made Sam so popular with the inmates? I asked a few guys why they had sent cards, some of whom were known as hard men and feared by many around the prison. Their answers were almost always the same: "Because Jaunty is sound; he makes sure we get our football; he's OK."

That's about as high a compliment any officer will get as far as inmates are concerned. It's true, you know: Sam got as much abuse shouted at him as any other officer, but underneath they respected him and it was at such a time as this they let him know that. If you were to ask Sam about it all, he would just shrug and say, "I don't know. I am only doing my job." So he was, but the way he did it showed he cared for men too, and we all knew that.

My life in prison was anything but dull! Once I got caught smuggling – a very serious offence in jail, you can get time added on to your sentence for this. Of course it depends on what one is smuggling; most times it is likely to be drugs or weapons. But it wasn't any of these I was caught with. I had just moved in to share a cell with 'Big D'. Many nights we would lay and sing choruses we had learnt in Reverend David Jardine's weekly Bible study. Sometimes we would forget some of the words but it never put us off. I remember thinking one night, *it would be great if we had two hymnbooks, we could sing to our heart's content*. It wasn't long after there was a riot in another part of the prison; prisoners on remand took over their wing in protest. It was a few days before things got restored to normal, but by this time a lot of the furniture was broken up and used as weapons by inmates. What they didn't break, the screws did – each cell was stripped bare and everything tossed out on to the landing. All this rubbish was dumped up in the garden to be eventually taken away to the city dump outside. There was a mountain of stuff, broken chairs, cupboards, beds, bookshelves etc. all laying in pieces. We were told by the officer in charge of us not to go near this part of the garden; it was off limits.

A few days later that I was told to go empty a wheel barrow of old cabbage foliage down in the dump. It was while I was down there I looked across at all this mountain of junk that I noticed a pile of red books lying scattered around the ground, it was a pile of the prison hymnbooks, called 'Redemption Hymnals'. I immediately thought to myself, if only I could get my hands on two of them. So I made a plan. I started to rake up any debris I could find around the garden just to get me back down to the dump again. Each time I made my way a little closer toward the junk pile. By my fourth or fifth journey I worked up close enough to the pile to be in reach of the hymnbooks. I had to time it right when the screw was looking away. I reached over and grabbed two of the hymnbooks and stuffed them inside my overalls. Everything went according to plan. I was feeling good with myself. A few moments later, I was walking back up again. Suddenly there was a shout, "Stop that prisoner!" A screw with a dog come running up towards us. He was panting, out of breath.

"Get up against the wire and spread your arms and legs, now," he said; both he and his dog were snarling. He started to talk through his radio to the control room, "Prisoner apprehended, beginning to search, over." He turned to the other officer who was my escort and said, "The security cameras up on the wall spotted him lifting something from the pile of junk and stuffing it inside his overalls, you should have been watching him more closely." The officer's face became very serious. "What was it?" he asked and he began to frisk me. Almost immediately he felt them. "Found something," he said, quite excited into the radio. "What is it?" the officer with me asked. I looked over my shoulder to see his face, he pulled out the two hymnbooks. Both screws looked at them in amazement; the dog handler was red-faced as he spoke into the radio. "It's, ugh, two hymnbooks, over." "Please repeat, over," was the immediate response from the control room. Again the officer said, "It's two flaming hymnbooks!" He brought me up to the officer in charge of the garden party.

In the office he said, "The cameras caught Hamilton

smuggling these," at that he tossed the two hymnbooks onto the table, "You deal with him," and with that he turned and walked out. "Auld Jaunty" (that is what we called the officer in charge of the garden) started to shout at me, a few moments later he stopped and said, "No more of this do you hear me, Hamilton?"

"I do. I am sorry about this," I answered.

"OK, now clear that table. It's time for tea. Call all the other men in." He turned and walked back into the small kitchen. I cleared the table as ordered, and lifted the hymnbooks again. I didn't know where to put them. I stuck them down the back of my trousers again! I was able to get them back to my cell without being caught.

That night we had a Holy Ghost party; we sang all night long. We sang every song with the same tune; if there were too many words we just skipped them and went on to the next line. We thought it was great! We were the only ones who thought that! Everyone else was up at their windows shouting at us to be quiet, we shouted back in between songs, "Any requests? Call them out!"

"The cameras caught Hamilton smuggling these," at that he tossed the two hymnbooks onto the table.

They all thought we were mad! We got to keep them, even during cell searches. The screws let them remain. Today, even now when I see one of those old Redemption hymnbooks it brings a smile to my face! I wonder if Paul and Silas had a Redemption hymnal when they sang all night in prison. God proved Himself more and more to me every passing day that he was interested in every aspect of my life.

Chapter Fifteen

MAKING A STAND

Since my conversion almost a year before, I began to talk to everybody, regardless if they were Loyalist or Republican, sex offender or thief, Protestant or Catholic. It made no difference, especially to God. This annoyed some folk, who got angry when they saw me talking to sex offenders and others I would have fought with before my conversion. Now I was trying to befriend them.

I remember two IRA men who I would speak to whenever I met them, though they never acknowledged me at any time and always looked away in disgust. This didn't bother me; I knew it would take a long time for most of the guys to accept me as a genuine Christian, especially Catholics. A few of them did at this time, but not these particular two.

It happened one day I was sitting outside in the exercise yard alone, reading my Bible, and these two guys were out walking around the yard. They had passed me a number of times but still up to that point had never talked to me. It was quite a surprise to me when one of them as he passed me by sat a sweet on top of my Bible! I looked up as they walked on by, and when they came around again, I said, "Thanks, I hope it's not poisoned." They laughed and stopped walking and one of them began to speak to me, and said, "I've been watching you to see if you really are one of these born again Christians."

"So what's your conclusion then?" I asked him.

"We think you're genuine; every time we see you, you're reading your Bible; you really do believe all that stuff," he said as he pointed to my Bible. That day was a turning point with them guys they always spoke to me from then on.

I had another experience with an IRA man about two years later and I remember it well. That particular morning, I was waiting to go out on my first parole home. This was my first three-day leave and that morning I was sitting in my cell with the cell door open waiting to be called. I looked up and was surprised when an IRA man came walking into my cell!

"You must be the happiest man in this prison, every time I see you, you have a smile on your face. Is it because you're a Christian, or what is it?" he asked.

"You're right first time Sean, that's what it is; it's because I know Jesus Christ personally," I answered with a smile on my face. "Is it OK to sit down?" he asked (he knew it's not the done thing, Protestant having a Catholic, or vice versa, in one's cell.) "It's no problem," I answered. "Sit down man." He went on to ask me, "How can you say, Davey, that you know Jesus, like, personally? No one can say that, not even the priest."

"Listen," I said, "you can, if you really want to. What I have, you can have also. Then you can know Him for yourself, that's what the Bible teaches us." I opened my Bible up to show him, and we talked for quite a while, he asking the questions and me trying to answer them. Then he said to me, "I would really love to have what you have, Davey."

"Sean," I replied, "you can have what I have, simply by asking Jesus to take your life over from today; it's that simple."

"But how?" he asked. I could see on his face he was really searching; he really wanted to know. I said to him, "If you want your life changed then repeat this prayer after me and make it your own prayer."

As I said the prayer out loud, he repeated it word for word. When I finished it, he looked up at me, his face was beaming, his eyes shining, we were both laughing.

When I got out of prison the first thing I did, was to go and buy a Bible for Sean. If someone had said on my first day back out of prison that's what I would do, I would have gone mad; Me! Buy a Bible for an IRA man! It sounds so far from reality I never could have imagined such a thing happening! But it did! (I have included this prayer at the end of this book, if you would like to know Jesus Christ personally, then turn to it now and pray it out aloud, and let God change your life today. Today can be the first day of the rest of your life not just a new start in life, but rather a new life to start from this day on!)

Today can be the first day of the rest of your life not just a new start in life.

Occasionally there are times when it is difficult as a Christian you have to make a stand. I guess one of my hardest trials was during a prison riot. Prison riots never really achieve anything. I had been involved in my fair share of them over the years, but it's worse when you're a Christian and there is one planned to come down, and you're stuck in the middle of it! That's just what happened. I was sitting in the dining hall having my lunch, when the guy sitting next to me said, "Don't get up from your chair, there is a protest planned, it's a sit-down, no one moves." I knew the rules OK: no one is allowed to get up and leave but if they do, how do you stop them? There are thieves, muggers, rapists, all kinds of guys in for all kinds of crimes, how do you stop them from leaving?

It's simple; someone came up with this idea; the first person who gets up to leave pays the price for everyone who wants to go. If a man moves from his table then the rule is everyone throws their steel tray at him, which leaves him in a mess, cut to pieces. Being bombarded by maybe a hundred steel trays is not a pretty sight. Only then are others free to leave, but the first is the sacrifice. No-one wants to be the first.

Being bombarded by maybe a hundred steel trays is not a pretty sight.

As I sat there, thinking about all this, I thought to myself, *this is all I need, how can I say I'm a Christian yet take part in a protest; this will destroy my witness, all the screws will say you're still a paramilitary when you obey their orders.* I started to pray; *Lord, show me what you want me to do.* I had no sooner prayed this in my mind, when suddenly I felt as if an unseen hand had taken hold of my collar and lifted me up out of my seat! I could not believe this was actually happening to me – here I was walking through all these tables towards the door, waiting for the trays to start flying! As I walked past the centre tables where all the top men sat — unofficially, it was here that most decisions were made by the paramilitaries – I looked over at these men. One of them spoke out, "It's not because Davey's afraid that he's walking out, but it's because he is a Christian."

No one moved, I continued walking toward the doors, I could see the riot squad standing alert ready for the order to rush in once the doors opened. I kept walking, I couldn't understand it. Why was nothing happening! My heart was still pounding! What's stopping them I thought! Seconds seem like hours, any second now they will all throw their trays. I was wrong; they never did, and I walked out the doors. Immediately others who were waiting for the chance to run jumped up because they knew I was the scapegoat, so they were free to go. In a matter of minutes the whole protest was over and everyone continued to leave the dining hall. It was over as quick as it started. Back in my cell, I lay on the bed looking up at the ceiling, "God don't do that again! It's not good for my health!" I shouted. But I knew He protected me, while one hand lifted me up the other was around me keeping me safe! I knew that was one experience I wouldn't forget in a hurry!

Two years later, one afternoon when I was working up in the prison garden, a short-term prisoner asked me a question. "Davey, did you ever stop a riot in the jail?" I was surprised by this question and asked him why he would ask me such a question. He said that during the lunchtime lock-up, two officers were standing idle, outside his cell-door talking. The conversation was overheard by this prisoner. One of them said, "Davey is not afraid to stand up as a Christian – remember when he stopped the riot in 'D' wing? He wouldn't have risked his life like that if he wasn't for real." I laughed; even the screws remembered it too!

Another time when I did something strange, or out of the ordinary, was when I was working as an orderly in the dining hall serving out the food. It happened that four men just came on to the wing that day after being sentenced for their involvement in a sex scandal which involved a boys' home in Belfast. It got a lot of media coverage, and lots of people were angry about it. These four men were sitting at a table in the dining hall when everyone got out for tea. They were getting all these dirty looks from everyone, and it was obvious they were frightened and afraid to move. As I was watching them I realised although they each had a dinner none of them had cutlery to eat it with. I was working behind the wire grill, so I walked over to the sink and got knives, forks and spoons for all of them. I then went to pass them through the wire to another prisoner and I asked him to pass them over to them, he looked at me and said, "You must be joking! They would all kill me" – he meant the other men there in the dining hall. So I turned to the screw and said, "Open the grill, and let me out." I then walked over to their table and gave each of them a set of cutlery. Everyone was watching, and then they all started to hiss at me. I got really angry and turned around and shouted, "These men are entitled to have a knife, fork and spoon, just like the rest of you! I don't expect you to eat your dinner with your fingers nor them either!"

I walked back to the grill and the screw hurriedly let me back in; he didn't know what to expect. It was amazing out of all the men there, only one man pulled me later about it. There was plenty of guys there who could easily have pulled my head off and thought nothing about it. That evening this particular guy came over to me and said he didn't like what

I had done, he was looking for a reaction from me. I wasn't afraid. I just smiled at him. He was a Catholic guy. I knew he didn't really want trouble; he was trying to act tough, waiting to see what I would do. I answered him by saying, "Jimmy I didn't do it to win favour of the month award, neither does it bother me what you or anybody else thinks about what I do. I try to do what I think is right. If you want to make something more out of it, it's up to you, man."

He was unsure about it, so he decided to let it drop at that, he just gave a shrug, turned and walked away. I was glad nothing more came of it. I never thought I would see the day I would risk my life to help sex offenders, looking back afterwards I said to myself, "Man, I've come a long way from wanting to burn them in the exercise yard!" The truth was I didn't see them now as any different from the rest of us, or any worse for that matter: none of us were better than anybody else, we all have broken the law – both man's and God's – and now we were all paying for it.

I knew he didn't really want trouble, he was trying to act tough, waiting to see what I would do.

Some of the things that happened to me while in prison, I know some people would find hard to believe. Like the time I was washing and I had a tattoo of the word 'SEX' in the middle of my right hand. As I was washing myself in the sink, I was throwing water over my face. I pulled out the plug and as the water began to turn down the plug-hole, I saw a word in the water; it was turning round and round, and I read the word 'SEX'! I immediately looked at my hand and my tattoo was gone! I turned to the guy beside me and said my tattoo just washed down the sink! He just turned and said, it must have been one of those rub on ones! He just laughed; he didn't believe me! I said to myself, "If you tell anyone else they will say you're mad!" I only shared that with a few people and even they laughed too! I learned that things sometimes happen that are better left untold!

The tattoo cleansing was one of many miracles that God has given me since he saved me from a wretched life. But the gift of salvation I know now to be the greatest miracle of all.

After I had served three years I was eligible for my first home leave, I had applied for it and was waiting to hear if it was granted. It was on Christmas Eve that the No.1 Governor decided to see me. (He was the man who ran the whole prison; there are governors for each wing.) I had been a Christian for over two years at that time and I hadn't been in any trouble since my conversion. I was surprised when told he wanted to see me; for one thing I hadn't expected to be called out into his own personal office. Standing in front of his desk, I looked at this man, the No.1 Gov. He was soon to retire – the sooner the better some said. He had a bad reputation from staff and prisoners alike, and I was soon to find the reason for this myself.

"As far as I am concerned you haven't changed any, you are not getting home leave!"

He looked up from reading my file and said, "Hamilton, your record in prison is excellent; you have been a good prisoner; it seems you work well in the kitchen and are studying to be a cook." I smiled at him and answered, "Yes sir." I thought to myself, *I am getting out on home leave here!* The Governor did not smile back but went on to say, "I also have been reading your police record from outside. It's atrocious, and as far as I am concerned you haven't changed any; you are not getting home leave! Out you go."

Our interview ended just as quick as that. I couldn't believe it. I was still standing looking at him, until the officer gave me a tug indicating for me to follow him out. The thought in my mind was, *I haven't changed any?* If only you knew, Governor... At least God knows and I know that I am a changed man – that's the important thing. It was a big disappointment for me not getting that Christmas leave.

Chapter Sixteen

CALLED TO THE MINISTRY

I had begun to study in prison for a few reasons; it was a good way to help pass the time and also to try and get a proper education, something I hadn't taken seriously before. I tried to complete one course each year I was in prison. In my final year I studied for an A Level course in religious studies. I was to sit the exam three months before my release. Because my mind was on passing this exam, it kept me from getting gate fever. I was glad when I got the result to say I'd passed it, my first A Level.

It was about two years before that I first was introduced to a man called James McIlroy. He came into the prison to sing and I found out he was the director of a Christian organisation called Prison Fellowship, not long started to work in the prisons of Northern Ireland. Although the work was fairly new in Ireland, it was already working in many other countries worldwide. It was founded by a man called Charles Colson, who was former special counsel to President Richard Nixon, and had spent seven months in prison for Watergate related offences.

It was upon his release from prison that this ministry was born in his heart. Today it is an international prison outreach and Chuck Colson is an internationally respected author and speaker. His books include *Born Again,* and *Life Sentence!* both of which I read while in prison. I never imagined then that years later, my own story would be included in one of his books, or that Chuck himself would come to visit me in Belfast prison.

James McIlroy became a regular figure around the prison, visiting men, not only in 'The Crumlin' but in other prisons in Northern Ireland as well. At first, I didn't know how to accept him. Like many guys I was suspicious of him, *One of these do gooders,* I thought. As time went by, I would hear guys talking about him – "He's OK." One guy told me he asked him to collect the money from the gate to go buy a present for his wife, and he did! That impressed me; not too many would go out of their way to go shopping for a prisoner's wife. Word soon got around he was for real; prisoners have a way of knowing who is genuine and who isn't. If there was a need that a prisoner had, as long as it didn't break any of the prison rules James would try to help. On one occasion a prisoner's wife couldn't get up to the prison to visit because of transport problems – James McIlroy solved the problem by driving her up to the prison, not just the once but for the next four years! Each week he would collect this woman and sometimes children too, drive them up to the prison and then sit outside and wait for them to take them home again and never once would he accept money offered towards his petrol costs.

I began to like this man and over the next few years we became good friends. I started to look forward to it when he came in to take part in the service in prison. I remember one particular day we were kept locked up because an officer had been murdered. As I was praying and reading my Bible that morning, I read something that seemed to jump out of the pages at me – Acts 26:16–18:

But rise, and stand upon thy feet: for I have appeared unto thee for this purpose, to make thee a minister and a witness both of these things which thou hast seen, and of those things in which I will appear unto thee; delivering thee from the people, and from the Gentiles, unto whom now I send thee, to open their eyes, and to turn them from darkness to light, and from the power of Satan unto God, that they may receive forgiveness of sins, and inheritance among them which are sanctified by faith that is in me.

I realised that God was speaking to me. This was a personal commission; what God wanted of me.

Even when I tried to carry on reading I kept feeling prompted to go back and read these verses over again. I realised that God was speaking to me. This was a personal commission; what God wanted of me. I remember the date well, it was the 16th of February 1982. The actual meaning puzzled me; did it really mean "a minister and a witness"? The witness part was OK for me, but this minister bit! What did God mean? A minister, like Batman! No way man; it couldn't be! I searched all the Bible commentaries I could find, but none gave me any real explanation.

It was only two days later when I learned the truth. I went to the Methodist service, where we were having a guest speaker that afternoon. His name was the Rev Derek Haskins and I remember as he got up to speak, he held up three pages of pink paper. "This is my sermon, that I had planned to speak, but I am not going to preach it, you will be glad to know. Instead I feel God wants me to tell you how I became

181

a minister." He went on to tell us how he had only a normal education, had left school early and started working in the shipyard in Belfast. It was there God called him out to go into full time ministry.

That afternoon I listened as this man answered every question that I had asked God just the few days before. I kept telling God all the reasons why I couldn't really be a minister, now I was listening to God telling me through this man, "You shall be!" If God says it then that's enough. I knew then deep down in my heart, God had a plan for my life, that I was called as a minister of the Gospel. It was then a warm peaceful feeling engulfed my heart.

I never would have considered it possible, never had such a thought even entered my head. It was far beyond me. But I thank God for it; there is no greater calling, no other

Nothing thrills me more than to be called into the ministry to serve my Lord Jesus Christ

profession, no other ambition that could satisfy me more, nothing thrills me more than to be called into the ministry to serve my Lord Jesus Christ. I knew that day I would not be going back to my trade ever again. But I didn't know what I would actually do upon my release. How God revealed His will for me to work for Prison Fellowship happened this way.

Time began to go faster it seemed. I eventually came down to my last year. My father began asking me, "What do you plan to do, work-wise, when you get released for good?" All I could say was, "I don't know yet Dad, God hasn't shown yet." He didn't know what to say in answer to this. Every visit he would ask the same question and I would answer, "I am still praying for God to show me." Poor Dad, he was doing everything in his power not to blow up on the visit!

It was a little time later, when I'd about eight months left to serve and I had been talking to the prison chaplain, Rev David Jardine. He told me he was praying about my release and what I should do afterwards in the way of work. He told me he was on the Executive Board of Prison Fellowship and felt I should consider working along James McIlroy. I smiled at that. By this time I knew James a lot better; we had talked a few times but I hadn't thought about us working together. "I will certainly pray about this and see what the Lord says to me about it," I said. That night I did just that. I asked the Lord to show me a sign, if this was His doing. As I read my Bible later on that evening, my attention was drawn to this verse, "I have opened a door for you no man can shut." My heart leapt, this is what I wanted to know! "Lord, can you give me another sign, just to confirm it?"

The following day I was working up in the garden cutting the grass, it was a good day and the afternoon sun was shining. I heard my name called – "Hamilton visit!" Now that was a surprise! I looked up to see an officer waiting to escort me back with him over to the main building, "You have an ecclesiastical visit," he shouted. As I walked down the hill towards the main building, I felt something within me say, *this day is a day you are going to remember.* I didn't know who it was that wanted to see me; it was a real surprise to see James McIlroy when I walked through the door into the visit cubicle.

After a few moments of general talk, James told me he had been at a meeting the night before and a lady spoke to him and suggested, "It would be better if there were an ex-prisoner who could work alongside you." As he travelled the long drive home that night, he said it seemed the words the woman spoke echoed around his ears, and it was my name and face he kept seeing before him. It touched him that much, he decided to come and see me the very next day. When he finished telling all this I laughed, "I supposed you were talking to David Jardine too?" I said, knowing what I thought to be the answer. "No" he said, "Why do ask that?" When he said no, I was shocked! I then told him what had happened the day before and how David had offered me the same job. Now it was his turn to be shocked!

We both knew then, this was God's doing. I said "Let me pray about this," (as if I needed to) it seemed to be the only thing to say. But I knew inside me this was God's doing. That night I couldn't wait to be in my cell alone, just to get talking to the Lord! After praying I started to read the Bible, and as usual God spoke to me through what I read. "I went unto Troas to preach the Gospel, and found a door opened unto me..." I just shouted "Praise God! Thank you Jesus!" and that was that. I knew the next step, that's all I need to know. At last I now knew what God wanted me to do once released. I remember thinking, *that will please my dad, just to get an answer on our next visit!*

As I hadn't much time left to serve, I had started to pray about my relationship with James McIlroy. Every day I prayed that I would be accepted by his family. James and I got on the best, but many times I wondered about his wife, *maybe she will have problems with me as an ex-prisoner.* James had said to me, "On your parole you can come and stay in my home in Randalstown." I just smiled, I was worried how would his wife find me – would she be suspicious of me, an ex-prisoner?

I remember meeting Margaret for the first time. She seemed very warm and friendly toward me, a beautiful lady who seemed to have no qualms about having ex-prisoners staying in her home. It soon became obvious to me Margaret was behind her husband in all that he did. She even asked me if I wanted a hot water bottle for bed! I laughed and said no thanks. She then told me to try not to waken her mum who slept in the room directly below my room and not to drop my shoes on the floor when I took them off. Although they were nursing her mother, they still had an open house and every one was welcomed there.

I liked that, I really felt accepted in James's home, and with his family too.

Later on as I got to know them better I found all of his sons and daughters were great, especially the twin girls, and were fully behind their dad in his work. The reason for this was that they each had a personal relationship with the Lord and they were a strong Christian family; the first Christian family I'd ever met. They had no suspicions toward me but readily accepted me and from that first night on we all became good friends. I lay in bed laughing to myself that night in James's house. I had no need to feel nervous. I knew God had answered all my prayers about this family.

They had no suspicions toward me but readily accepted me.

My next parole didn't go according to plan. I was planning to go out to attend a Prison Fellowship world conference and spend the weekend with Charles Colson. It so happened that a week before I was with an officer working up the garden. I remember it started to pour out of the heavens; torrents of rain. I had been working down on my knees planting rose buds, so we ran for cover underneath a doorway. It was then this officer said to me, "Why have you stopped working? Go back out and carry on, I will stand here and watch you." I looked at him to see if he was joking. He wasn't. "Mister, I will get pneumonia if I go out in that rain to work," I replied. He just said, "You will get wet, not me. Now get back to work." I got angry and saw red, "Is that right, well I've news for you I won't get wet either, because I am refusing to work."

I was banged up all weekend! It was the talk of the jail.

He threatened to take me to 'the boards.' I just answered, "Let's go now then," and stepped out into the rain. I didn't care about 'the boards.' Ten minutes later I was banged up in the punishment block. It was only then I began to think, *is this really happening to me? This is crazy!* He probably will come back in ten minutes and let me out again. He didn't. I was banged up all weekend! It was the talk of the jail.

Even other officers came in to see me, they couldn't believe it either. They told me the officer who charged me for refusing to work was a rookie – that is, he was only in the job about a week and I was his first charge. It was Monday before I knew the Governor would come to see me and sure enough, my door opened and in he walked. This was the wing governor and he was the man I'd asked for to have the baptism service in the bathhouse, a few months before.

"What's this I hear Hamilton, that you refused to work? Tell me it's not true."

"I am afraid sir, it is," I replied. I went on to tell him the whole story, but of course the officer had told a different story, he just forgot to say about it raining at the time! The Governor then said to me, "I suppose the devil made you do this, Hamilton?" I answered, "No sir, the devil had nothing to do with this, it was just between your officer and me and I didn't like his attitude." He looked at me and smiled slightly. "And I don't like your behaviour, your parole is cancelled." I was stunned – I wasn't expecting this – no parole! I had been reading a Bible that was in the cell when the Governor walked in. I had my finger in it still to keep my place as I sat down after he had gone. I immediately began to pray, "God, you can over-rule this man, and get me my parole back for Monday." I looked down at the Bible and the last four words on the page said: "No, I will not." I could not believe it! You can't even argue with that! Well you can, but it does you no good! God and I argue all the time, but He always wins!

Two days later I was reading my Bible, while waiting for my door to open to let me out for church. Although on punishment, we still got out for church. But I knew I would be separated from everybody else. I'd be up in the balcony sitting with an officer. While sitting reading in Matthew 7 about the wise and foolish builders. I noticed that the trials were exactly the same for both guys regardless of the one guy being a Christian. So I said to the Lord, "That's not fair: the foolish guy, he deserves it, but not the wise guy. Why should he have the trials?" I believe God spoke to me in my mind and said, "Why not? Just because he believes in the Lord, do you think then he should walk around with the sun shining on him while it rains on everyone else?"

The truth is we all go through the trials and storms of life, but for the Christian the outcome is different because he knows the Bible says that "All things work together for good to them that love God" (Romans 8:28). Sometimes we cannot see how this is possible, but the Bible teaches that we *know* we have God's assurance, as we are standing on the rock. God is with us in every trial. Tough times don't last, but tough people do!

The Bible teaches that we KNOW we have God's assurance, as we are standing on the rock.

This revelation blessed me, next thing I knew my door opened, and was locked back. "Combined Service!" the officer shouted as he passed by to open the next cell. I walked behind the officer and climbed the spiral staircase which led to the prison chapel. I was sitting alone, back at the door; two officers were standing talking together. I could see all the boys sitting down below me, everyone was talking and shouting across the aisle, the chaplain hadn't come out of the vestry yet to start the service. I wondered who would be taking the service this morning.

It was the Revd Jackson Buick, the new Presbyterian minister who had replaced Bill Vance. He was a small man in stature but what he lacked in height, he made up for in courage and stamina. He had a heart like a lion. But that first morning as he reached the lectern and stood up on it, he could barely see over the top. He stood up on his toes and looked over the top and said, "I don't know if I am to preach over this or under it!" The place erupted with laughter. The boys liked his humour. I enjoyed his preaching a lot. We soon became good friends.

I was sitting up in the balcony waiting to hear what his sermon would be this particular morning. He opened the Bible and the boys all quietened down. A few moments later he began to read, "The wise man builds his house upon the rock." I just felt a surge within me and before I could stop myself I yelled at the top of my voice, "Hallelujah!" The two officers beside me almost jumped out of their skin! Everyone sitting down below turned around and looked up at me. I put my fist up in the air and shouted "Hallelujah!" again. One of the guys shouted out, "Davey is crazy!" Jackson looked up at me gave me a smile and carried on with his reading. I was thrilled and knew God wanted me to remember what he had shown me earlier that morning!

Chapter Seventeen

STEPPING OUT IN FAITH

I had found out an old mate of mine outside had also got converted. He started to visit me occasionally. Neither of us could have ever imagined then we would later become in-laws. Billy Smith was Sharon's brother. Often I would put out a visit pass for him and his wife. On one occasion, Billy's wife couldn't make it up and so Sharon came up instead. This was the first time I had seen her in years. I knew that she had been living with her brother for the past few years, since the break-up of her first marriage.

I enjoyed it when she came up to visit me. But I never thought any further than that. I didn't think she would be interested in forming a relationship with me; I knew years ago she had a crush on me, but she was just a young teenager then.

Sharon's Story continued:

My life was just a sham. I started going out clubbing, trying to enjoy myself, but although I was smiling outside I was far from being happy. My smile was just a complete cover up for how I really felt inside. Looking back I was just putting on a show. That's how it went on for the next lot of years. When I was 21, my brother's marriage broke up and he came to live with me in my flat. I enjoyed having him around, he

191

would often mind the child for me when I wanted to go out with my mates. One Saturday afternoon, on my way home with a friend we were walking along the main road when we met a man giving out gospel tracts. We knew who he was, he was the talk of the whole area where we lived. He was a converted terrorist, in the same organisation and in fact the same squad that David belonged to. He had got converted while in prison and is now released.

As we went to pass by him he gave my friend a tract, I tried to walk on but he offered me one too. I took it and just stuck it in my pocket, I didn't want to have it, but I couldn't throw it away in case he was watching. I forgot about it. When it came time for my friend and I to separate, we agreed to meet again that evening to go out for a drink and maybe look for a few boys.

My brother had agreed the night before that he would babysit for me. At home I walked into the kitchen and put the kettle on for a cuppa. It was then I remembered the tract that Davy had given me so I pulled it out to look at it. It actually was a small booklet entitled, *What Must I Do To Be Saved?* What's this about? I wondered. I started to read it, while I was waiting for the kettle to boil. I hadn't read very far into it – I realised it was speaking to me – it was strange, it was stirring

It was strange, it was stirring something up in my heart. I just knew it was The Truth I was reading.

something up in my heart. I just knew it was The Truth I was reading. It was so obvious, all that it said about life I was agreeing with. I didn't realize it but it was convicting me more and more as I read on. I started to think, *I need to check this out, that this is real, this is right.*

I read a few pages more when I read a statement, "You are a sinner, you need the Lord Jesus more than you need anything else in the world." It went on to explain the way of salvation. A battle began to rage inside me; it all came home to me how bad I really was. I was reasoning all these things, it's right. I thought this is impossible for me to change. I cannot stop smoking even. I don't think I can do anything to change but I want to. There were other things too I would have to give up that weren't right in my life.

I know I can't do this but I am going to ask God to change me anyway.

The moment I did ask, something happened, I immediately knew and started to cry and laugh tears of joy and I found an immediate relief! I read the rest of the tract. It just happened – I was born again. It was done, I knew it had happened! I went to see my friend and told her and thought that she would be surprised. But she knew what a Christian was. I thought that I was going up to tell her but her sister was a Christian. I told her I wouldn't be drinking anymore and went back home.

Billy didn't come home that evening although he was meant to. The next morning when I opened my eyes I knew I was different. I went into Billy's bedroom with a cup of tea to tell him the news. Billy thought he was going to get a telling off. He looked guilty, but I was smiling, really smiling (probably the first real smile ever.) He perked up and said, "Did you go out last night?" I said, "No Billy I will never be out that way again. I got saved yesterday afternoon."

He realised it was all very serious and real and tried to join in. He said he knew some Christians and could get in touch with some people of the same mind. I said OK and he went about his business. On Monday morning my friend told me she had talked to her sister and that she had talked to her pastor and told him that her sister's friend had got saved on her own on Saturday afternoon. The pastor was interested. He asked, "Could I come with a girl from the church to see me?" I said yes, "That's OK." So on Monday night this man arrived called Pastor Johnson with a young woman, Pauline. They came in; I made them tea; he opened the Bible. "This is for you." Acts 2 verse 41. "They that gladly receive his word."

So that was it. It sounded good and I needed to go to meetings. He kindly came for me to take me to meetings. He came a considerable distance, for quite a while. Billy eventually got in touch with his friends but I told him there was no need. Looking back now I believed that God protected me for I found out that they were Jehovah's Witnesses.

Billy began to study to find what this religion was all about. Who was right? But I said, "That's not what to do. You get saved first and God will do the rest."

But he wouldn't listen to me. As always, he was trying to put me right.

Eventually he went to a meeting with Pastor Johnson, got convicted, fell down on his knees and called out to God. He got saved – went back to his wife again. Roberta started coming to the meetings and she got saved too! She was a chain smoker and stopped.

Then one day Billy got a letter from prison from David Hamilton. Billy said to me, "That's a letter from David

Hamilton. You'll not believe this but he's a Christian now too." My immediate thought was, *Imagine David Hamilton a Christian and me a Christian.* I started thinking we could be together – then I suddenly thought – *that's ludicrous, that could never happen.* I'm glad no one knew what I was thinking!

For the next few years I went to every meeting that it was possible for me to go to. I was just absorbing the things of God and seeking to put them into practice in my life.

I then moved into my brother's house in Rathcoole, with him and his wife. She was expecting their second child at the time. God directed my thoughts and He was making me reflect on things in my past; about relationships. I thought of my ex-husband, God challenged me, was I thoughtful for his salvation? I had had no contact with him at all for quite a few years. The very next morning my sister-in-law handed me a letter from him. I could not believe it! So I visited him in prison and brought Louise, she was then 7 years old. She didn't go near him. He couldn't understand why I was still single. I told him it was my relationship with God which was the most important thing in my life. God was doing something else but it wasn't what people thought. They were trying to sort our relationship out, but both of us knew it wasn't to be.

Next thing I heard was that David and his wife were planning to get divorced. I was really burdened for David's wife and began to pray she would get converted and save their marriage. So I started taking her to gospel meetings. But she never responded. She continued to live with this other man. The divorce went through six months later.

I began to think about David Hamilton a lot. One day

when I was praying, I told the Lord how I felt about David. God spoke to my heart and told me I would marry him in four years' time! I was not to mention it to another living soul, but to wait and watch Him bringing us together! I was totally amazed by all this! I still had not seen him in years. We had had no contact whatsoever ... Not long after this David began to send out visitors' passes to Billy and Roberta. On one of these occasions Roberta couldn't go, so I went instead. But when I saw him I felt the same

God spoke to my heart and told me I would marry him in four years' time!

way about him as I did all those years ago. At the end of our visit David kissed me and I walked down the road afterwards still feeling that kiss on my cheek. I didn't wash for a week after that kiss!

I started to visit David regularly, never on my own, always with Billy and Roberta. Then when he got out on parole for three days he came to visit us. Eventually late in the evening Billy and Roberta went to bed. This was the first occasion of our being alone together. It was then he asked me if I would date him when he was released! I was overjoyed. God's promise was coming to pass. When he returned to prison again I wrote and visited him for last year of his sentence. After his release, we were married seven months later.

Back to David's story:

I was glad it was in my last six months when I started to fall in love with Sharon. I enjoyed being around her, all we would talk about on our visits was the Lord. I decided if I were to married again it would be to a woman who had these same qualities about her. I honestly never thought before about marrying Sharon – simply because I'd known her for so long and since we were teenagers living next door to each other.

It was during my second parole I went to visit her brother and it was later on that night he decided to go on to bed and handed us a cup of tea each before he went up! This was the first time I had ever been alone with her, before we were always in the company of others. We sat and talked into the early hours of the morning. We drank so much tea we eventually had to go out looking to buy some milk about six o'clock in the morning. By that time I was hooked on her!

I went back into prison with her photograph in my Bible. I was showing all my mates her picture, "See my girlfriend, guys." When they looked at the photo they said, "But that's the girl who has been coming up to visit you regularly, was she not your girl then?" I said, "No, we were just good friends." They laughed, "Sure, just good friends was that all?" They didn't believe me!

I had a wonderful experience a few weeks later. One evening before lights out I was lying in bed looking at some photographs of Sharon and her little daughter Louise. As I was looking at Louise's photograph I had another experience from the Lord: suddenly it was as if gallons of love were poured into my heart for this little girl, and I began to cry for her. I fell in love with her too; she was a special gift because God had given her also to me. She became my daughter that night and so I wrote a letter and told her so. As I was in love those last few months seemed to go slow now. Seven months after my release Sharon and I got married.

By fasting and prayer I learned to know when God was speaking to me. I found the Bible to be alive to me; truly it is a living Word! No matter what I needed the answer to, somehow God would show me during these times what His will and purpose was. I developed such a hunger for the word of God, even the chaplain told me I was reading it too much! I have been known to sit up all night and read. I still do it; there are days I do nothing else but sit and read for hours on end, maybe six hours at a time. I never sit down to read without a pen, rule and paper. I like to underline my Bible as I read it; many verses in my Bible are dated when God has spoken through them to me at that particular time.

One occasion while in the Spirit, God spoke and told me that a preacher was coming in to speak at a service and he would have a special word for me. I was told a few days later that a team from the Christian Renewal Centre from Rostrevor were coming to minister to us. I was excited about this because I knew something was going to happen.

The Christian Renewal Centre was founded by Cecil and Myrtle Kerr in 1974 as an Oasis of peace amidst the violence of Northern Ireland, a community where Protestants and Catholics come together in reconciliation. It's a place I've visited many times since coming out of prison. Rostrevor is situated on the border between Ulster and the Irish Republic; to me it symbolises the white flag of neutrality between the orange and the green. I remember that Sunday well; The Rev Cecil Kerr lead a team of men and women as they ministered in various ways with the use of drama and song. Then Cecil shared a message with us; as he spoke I was listening really attentively in case I missed what God wanted to say. Well the service ended, and still I hadn't got anything out of it! Even if he sneezed I wrote it down! I got nothing out of it, man was I disappointed until Cecil did something really strange. By this time men were walking out of the chapel. Cecil shouted to the officer, "Hold it one moment! Ask those men to come back in again, I feel God is prompting me to say something to someone in here. It seems the unlikeliest of places but God is speaking to a man here today who he will use as an evangelist outside; he may not be another Billy Graham, but he will win many people to Jesus Christ."

"God is speaking to a man here today who he will use as an evangelist outside."

I couldn't believe it! I almost started to cry, I had to really brace myself to stop me from doing so. Somebody looked over at me and shouted, "That's Davey he's talking about!" I was hoping for a word but not something so explicit as this, I couldn't wait to get out of there!

Back in my cell a few moments later, another Christian friend came running in, "That was powerful Davey!" he said.

I couldn't even answer, all I did was sit on the bed and only then did I start to cry! This was one of the greatest experiences of my Christian walk. Even now when I look back I see that prophecy fulfilled, 14 years later! Since coming out of prison, I have seen thousands of souls saved, in many different countries. God has provided for me in miraculous ways and has given me the opportunity to preach His Gospel on Satellite television and to visit many cities and towns all over Europe, from the borders of the Ukraine in the East to Los

Angeles in the West of the United States of America. What a mighty God we serve!

I will never forget hearing the words: "Hamilton time served" to be walking across the prison yard for the last time. I had watched others for years step out to freedom, and now it was my turn. Some officers shouted farewell to me; I smiled and waved. It was with a mixture of emotions; I was leaving some guys in there I had come to love as brothers, and yet I was walking out to a new life.

Davey Hamilton the Terrorist was dead and it was now Davey Hamilton the Evangelist going out the gate. I knew I would never do time again. I was wondering what would happen in my life now, I didn't know what it was like to live as a Christian outside.

Those first few months were really hard; at times I thought it would be easier in jail. Getting used to carrying money around, being able to open and close doors for myself, learning to eat off a plate instead of a steel tray, turning lights on and off for myself – all those little things people take for granted. Even finding out I could have free medical prescriptions: I naturally assumed I had to pay for them, which I did. I was not long going back to the chemist and asking if I could have my money back as I didn't know about unemployment benefits.

"Davey Hamilton the Terrorist was dead and it was now Davey Hamilton the Evangelist going out the gate."

Then there was the Terrorist group too. I knew I had to face them, sure enough. I wasn't long out when I had a visit from one of them. The UVF Commanders wanted to see me. I was told to be at a bar in Belfast on such on such a date. I was told, "Make sure you're there – we don't want to have to go looking for you." I was not going to try and hide or take off somewhere. "I'll be there," I told him. I didn't tell any of my family, apart from my brother. He said he would come with me, "You can't go alone," he said. I told him. "I will not be alone, God will be there with me so I am not worried." He was afraid for me.

I had thought about this many times before in jail. Now this was it. I thought of what I would say to them. I knew one man already from my old UVF team who had been shot dead. He had become a Christian and tried to leave. I was leaving, no matter what. My mind was already made up. I was finished with it all. If they shoot me I will be in glory. I thought about that. I had no fear, none at all.

Friday arrived. We set off; my brother was telling me: "If you're not out in such and such a time I will call the police." It was obvious who was the more afraid – naturally, because at that time he was not yet converted. Today he is also a minister of the gospel. Praise God! Driving along I thought back to the time I first came to this bar to join them. I had really believed it was a cause worth dying for, but Jesus had given me a new cause, a cause worth living for. I decided the gospel of Jesus Christ is the only cause worth dying for. I was ready to die if that was the case. I could do nothing else. There was no other choice for me. I saw it quite clear cut, I had given my life to Christ, I could not deny him.

We stopped across the road from the bar. I said to my brother,

"Here goes," and jumped and ran across the road through the door into the bar … but that's another story.

POSTSCRIPT

I feel it's only proper to add a point here which is worth noting, and it is this: The prison system today is no longer the same as it was in my day. It has completely changed in Northern Ireland since my release. There has been much reform.

Today it is altogether different. You do not have to call the screws 'Sir.' There is no more having to work during the day, there are no more lock-ups during the day. You are allowed to go over to other wings to visit. The screws don't even come down the wings any more, they just call out your name and wait for you. Nowadays it's all on first name terms for officers and prisoners alike. You can have television in your cell, three or four can lock-up in the big cell together and watch movies all night long.

Today a lot of prisoners are into the drugs, in my day we made the home brew with all the fruit. Not anymore. It's the dope which is the thing now and it's increasing.

Of course there are good points about it as well. For instance the visits are far better; not just a table beside each other like in the old days, there is more privacy now. Back then the visit lasted half an hour once a week, and many times you were lucky even to get that. Nowadays, a visit could last possibly two hours if things are not too busy.

Having said all that, prison is still prison regardless of privileges. It's the loss of freedom that cannot be replaced.

Prison is always hard, regardless of how long the stay. It seems the longer one does the harder it is to get it out of one's mind. It can take some men years to learn to cope with life on the outside again. Others remain institutionalised.

I've come to realise prison leaves scars, some of which remain tender for a long time. Others, it seems, never really heal properly. Today this story is far from finished; my conversion in prison reads only as an introduction to what God continues to do in my life up until now. If the truth be told, what has happened to me since my release, God leading me on to greater heights and new fresh personal experiences of His wonderful grace and abounding love, far exceeds the story of my life prior my conversion.

Of course my salvation is something I will never cease to be thankful for. Over the years I've found out that salvation is truly the greatest miracle of all. But there is an onward journey, a pressing on to know Him more. We serve a merciful God, a God of Love, who gave me life, a reason for being, a life I have found to be truly in abundance, something the world can never give and, praise God, neither can it take away. Truly there is only one cause worth dying for, because it's only in dying in Christ that we are born to eternal life, but until that moment: I have a cause worth living for!

Conclusion

A CAUSE WORTH LIVING FOR

"Terrorist" – the word strikes fear in every country in the world now. Perhaps it has become the most important and frightening of all topics; so much so, that as I write in 2021, the British Army is at full stretch fighting bloody wars against Global Terror in far-flung lands.

Making us scared is in fact the terrorists' intention. We are all by now well aware of the effects terrorism has had on innocent travellers, whether by train or bus. As for air travel, the threat is so severe it has forced airline companies and airports to implement massive security measures. The media keep this threat real to us, with all the hype too. It's now become a key theme in thrillers and Hollywood movies.

What motivates terrorists? One size will not fit all, but many consider the Troubles in Northern Ireland to have arisen from conflicting religious terrorisms: Protestants fighting Roman Catholics. Certainly, religion fanned the flames that kept things ablaze. This is not just an Irish thing, as many as half of the world's thirty most dangerous terrorist groups claim religion as their motivation. Many experts in this field see religious terrorism as perhaps the world's most dangerous type, because it is the most dedicated and unpredictable, verging on fanaticism.

Ask religious terrorists themselves, however, and they probably won't own such a label; they prefer to see themselves as devout, fundamentalist, true believers in the religion of their fathers: at most, spiritual militants. They claim a divine command for their terror campaigns. It is regarded as the "neglected duty" and implied, directly or indirectly, in the sacred texts, or at least in their interpretation of them. This has come to be known in the west as "Jihad" or Holy War against an overpowering enemy, demonized as "The Great Satan". Such religious ideology, with its use of this martyrdom notion and the claim of spiritual rewards afterwards, encourages wannabe suicide bombers and discourages defectors. This makes religious terrorism altogether different to other forms of terrorism. Neither military nor diplomatic solutions have any worthwhile effect. Ceasefires and negotiations are of no consequence.

The ultimate nightmare is that weapons of mass destruction get into the hands of such religious terrorists – these people have no fear of destroying themselves and everybody else in the process. What's the answer? Is there a solution? Many are fearful there aren't any. But then my own mother thought I would never change, that I was totally committed to a cause which I thought was worth dying for.

God showed me that taking up arms for Loyalist Protestantism could never be right in His sight, for Jesus had already won the victory in my place. It was not a case of me deciding to defect from the cause – that's asking for trouble – but of God intervening and changing my heart. He transformed my life and totally changed my way of thinking and doing. I have come to trust God and depend on him. It was only then I found real peace, lasting peace.

Even as you finish reading this book, you may be fearful about your own life, about the circumstances of your loved ones or even the risk of worldwide disaster. I don't know what the future holds, but I know One who does. He understands. 2000 years ago, Jesus foretold that fear would be a common characteristic of the end of the age. It is popular in this day and age to treat the Bible as a storybook containing myths and fables, but all those willing to read it without prejudice see that Jesus' predictions are proving to be absolutely true, they are coming to pass. "Men's hearts failing them for fear and for expectation of those things that are coming on the world." (Luke 21:26).

But God says to those who put their trust in Him, "neither fear ye their fear" (Isaiah 8:12, KJV). Bible-believing Christians are aware of what's going on in the world today, they know what to expect, and know they have a safe refuge because they have a personal faith in God's Son, the Lord Jesus Christ.

Throughout the Bible the words of God are found time and time again saying to those who love Him and keep his commandments "Fear not for I am with you" (Isaiah 41:10, NKJV). Even in the valley of the shadow of death, David could say "I will fear no evil; For you are with me" (Psalm 23:4).

So if you have fear, I invite you to listen to Jesus as he says "Come to me, all you who are weary and burdened, and will give you rest." (Matthew 11:28, NIV).

If you have trusted Christ through reading this book, please write and tell us. If you would like further help please contact me via the publisher. On the next page, you will find some steps covering the way of salvation.

- Believe Christ is your friend and that He cares about you [1 Peter 5:7].

- Call upon Him for help—right now [Matthew 11:28-30].

- Believe Him to save you from your sin, depression and fear [Romans 10:9].

- Confess Him publicly as your Lord and Saviour [1 John 4:15].

- Believe He will cleanse you and make you a new person [2 Corinthians 5:17].

- Simply trust Him with childlike faith [Ephesians 2:8].

A SIMPLE PRAYER OF FAITH

Lord Jesus Christ, with my mouth I confess my sins, my selfishness, in living my own way and not your way. Please forgive me; wipe my slate clean and give me a new life to begin. I renounce the devil and all his ways and here and now I receive Christ as Lord of my life. Fill me with your Holy Spirit, give me a hunger to read the Living Word of God and teach me how to pray. Thank you, Lord, for answering my prayer; in Jesus' name I pray.

Amen